The Adolescent and Adult Neuro-diversity Handbook

by the same author

Asperger Syndrome and Employment
What People with Asperger Syndrome Really Really Want
ISBN 978 1 84310 677 7

Love, Sex and Long-Term Relationships
What People with Asperger Syndrome Really Really Want
Foreword by Stephen M. Shore
ISBN 978 1 84310 605 0

Asperger Syndrome and Alcohol
Drinking to Cope?
Matthew Tinsley and Sarah Hendrickx
Foreword by Temple Grandin
ISBN 978 1 84310 609 8

of related interest

Asperger Syndrome and Anxiety
A Guide to Successful Stress Management
Nick Dubin
Foreword by Valerie Gaus
ISBN 978 1 84310 895 5

The Adolescent and Adult Neuro-diversity Handbook

Asperger Syndrome, ADHD, Dyslexia, Dyspraxia and Related Conditions

Sarah Hendrickx

with a chapter on dyslexia by Claire Salter

Jessica Kingsley Publishers
London and Philadelphia

First published in 2010
by Jessica Kingsley Publishers
116 Pentonville Road
London N1 9JB, UK
and
400 Market Street, Suite 400
Philadelphia, PA 19106, USA

www.jkp.com

Library of Congress Cataloging in Publication Data
Hendrickx, Sarah.
    The adolescent and adult neuro-diversity handbook : Asperger's syndrome, ADHD, dyslexia, dyspraxia, and related conditions / Sarah Hendrickx.
        p. ; cm.
    Includes bibliographical references.
    ISBN 978-1-84310-980-8 (alk. paper)
    1. Autism spectrum disorders--Handbooks, manuals, etc. 2. Attention-deficit hyperactivity disorder--Handbooks, manuals, etc. 3. Adolescence--Handbooks, manuals, etc. 4. Adult--Handbooks, manuals, etc. I. Title.
    [DNLM: 1. Child Development Disorders, Pervasive. 2. Adolescent. 3. Adult. 4. Attention Deficit Disorder with Hyperactivity. 5. Communication Disorders. 6. Education. 7. Employment. WM 140 H4985a 2010]
    RC553.A88H4618 2010
    616.85'88200835--dc22

                                                        2009025645

British Library Cataloguing in Publication Data
A CIP catalogue record for this book is available from the British Library

ISBN 978 1 84310 980 8

Printed and bound in the United States by
Thomson-Shore, 7300 Joy Road, Dexter, MI 48130

Contents

Acknowledgements

I would like to thank all of those who have kindly contributed their time and expertise to helping me with this book, especially those who have honestly and openly shared their experiences as people affected by neuro-diversity in its many forms. For me, they make the theory stuff meaningful, for the understanding of how diagnostic criteria actually affect a person's life is surely the point of increased knowledge and research?

Grateful thanks go to the following for advice, proofreading, contributions and general support. Linnea Larson, Russ Fowler, Kit Spink, Allie Powell, Janet Taylor, Matt Tinsley, Susan L. Dunn Morua, Claire Salter, Sam Griffiths, Fiona Prior, Dr Hugh Rickards, Anna Caig. I am always surprised and overwhelmed by the willingness of both professionals and individuals to share their knowledge and personal experiences so readily. Thank you very much.

Embrace diversity!

Introduction

Diagnosed as an adult with dyslexia and a hint of attention deficit hyperactivity disorder (ADHD) at the age of 33 (after working as a dyslexia support tutor for a number of years), agoraphobia with panic disorder, a dash of obsessive-compulsive disorder (OCD) thrown in for good measure and a host of motor and vocal tics as a child – a few of which remain – I know how it feels to grow up with a sense of being 'odd' (and told so often enough), but with no explanation for that oddness. This meant that surely it couldn't be anything other than my own fault for deliberately being 'difficult', 'neurotic', 'weird' and a raft of other less than complimentary descriptors. When I think of the amount of neuro-diverse behaviours that I have had myself – which I hadn't really done so until I came to write this introduction – it comes as no surprise to me that I feel an affinity with, and ended up in, this area of work!

The term 'neuro-diversity' encompasses a range of developmental, neurological conditions and represents those who are, in some way, 'atypical' and who experience the cognitive and sensory world in a 'different' way. As mentioned above, I belong to this group myself.

Due to increasing understanding and research into the area of neurological and developmental conditions, opportunities for early assessment, diagnosis and support are increasingly available for children and young people, creating better informed and supported future generations. Unfortunately, those who were 'missed' as children or who grew up before all of this research had taken place may have had no diagnosis, a late one, or a wrong one, and received little or no guidance or information. Current study and research still tend to focus more on children and how they are affected by these conditions, with less dedicated to adults, who have different challenges to deal with. These conditions show themselves differently in adults; ADHD adults may no longer break their toys and jump on the furniture, but may instead struggle to keep focus in a business meeting or burn out due to having three jobs which they need to consume their excess of mental energy.

This book is therefore focused on how neuro-diversity displays itself in young people and adults, rather than young children. It is for medical practitioners, teaching professionals, counsellors and others who come into contact with individuals who 'just don't quite fit' or where you 'can't put your finger on what it is about him/her but there's something not quite right' and are looking for some framework or reference point to define these behaviours. It seeks to aid the path to the right support or the first clue as to what might be the cause of the difficulties and possibly unfulfilled life that the person has experienced. It is a reference guide to spot the indicators of a range of conditions complete with some ideas about what to do about them in a practical sense.

It is also written for those either already diagnosed or those looking for something which might serve as an initial explanation for their behaviour, difficulties they may have had, who they are and why life has worked out the way it has. It is also for family members and partners to learn more about how their loved ones tick and reassure them that their characteristics are real and need accommodating.

I hope it is positive in tone, because from my perspective, I wouldn't be rid of my neuro-diverse brain if I could. It provides me and those around me with endless amusement as I mispronounce words (and make up my own), get lost in buildings (ending up in men's toilets with alarming regularity – too many doors when you exit the ladies') and come up with an unending stream of crazy ideas, which get forgotten and replaced if they don't come to fruition within the blink of an eye. I watch 'normal' people with curiosity; people who are motivated by different things (social conformity being one of them) and whose brains seem to be taking an entirely different path to mine. I have not yet ceased to be amazed by this difference, which is apparent to me every day. I appreciate that some conditions are easier to live with than others and that there are those who don't feel 'blessed' by their diversity and would, given the choice or a magic pill, get rid of their disabilities in an instant. I hope that awareness, diagnosis and the understanding of others will at least make life more bearable in the mean time. For those people, appropriate treatments are covered in this book where they exist.

Specific medication is not discussed in detail as there are so many different options, the suitability of which will vary widely according to the individual and how they are affected. The cocktail of neuro-diversity and its accompanying stressors varies so much from person to person, there can be no cure-all that fits everyone. It may take trials of several medications or combinations of medications to find something which meets the person's needs. There is debate regarding medication and the extent of its effectiveness for a number of these conditions. Prevailing opinion on this subject changes frequently with new research developments and knowledge which highlight different issues. This book would be out of date before it reaches print. Professional medical advice should be sought to determine the most appropriate treatment.

I am fortunate to live and work in an environment where I am (mostly) accepted and/or tolerated and I know this is not the case for everyone. I began working as a Learning Support Assistant in a college, supporting students with a range of disabilities and diversity, and so have been taught to work with the difference, rather than to fight it. I wasn't fully aware at that time how much I had in common with some of my students.

That learning took place a few years later and the enormous positive impact it had on me has led me to believe that self-knowledge and self-confidence are the key to self-acceptance and in being able to present ourselves as who we are without apology as there is nothing wrong with us to apologize for. I am convinced that this late-life explanation of why I was constantly considered to have 'under-achieved', or thought of as simply 'lazy', despite having so much 'potential' as a child (an intelligence quotient (IQ) of 150+, never scored an A in any exam, failed to complete a university degree and a lifetime of under-employment and low income) has enabled me to find my strengths and make a late start. I have since written four books on Asperger syndrome and am achieving the highest marks possible for work on a master's degree in autism (due to the patience and unlocking of the mystery of critical evaluation by my tutor, Dr Nick Hodge – I am eternally grateful). I now work with my dyslexia and my impetuous nature, rather than against it. I will not proofread this book as I know I cannot maintain attention or recognize errors of spelling, grammar or sense. I get other people to do that for me. I will try to plan a schedule which means I will diligently write 5000 words per month over a period of months meaning a calm and stress-free progression to a finished manuscript. In reality, I will spend five months working out what I will do in my head, becoming increasingly stressed as the deadline looms and I have not managed to sit down long enough to write anything, then write the whole thing in two weeks, alongside running my own business, a second job, parenting and researching a master's dissertation. That's just the way my brain works and I kind of like it because I don't know anyone else who can do that, although I'm sure that some of you reading this will be able to do this and more. The downside isn't so great with constant high levels of stress and anxiety, some of which causes physical ill health, and an inability to just sit and relax while there are 'things that need to be done'.

I would like this book to allow some people to learn that they are not 'stupid', 'difficult' or to blame for their experiences or behaviour by realizing that there is a reason for why they are who they are. This does not mean that a label or a syndrome becomes an excuse not to move forward and challenge these difficulties. Knowledge of ourselves should help us to find strategies to cope with some of the issues, avoid a few others and simply accept a few more. Everyone has their oddness; it's just that some people have a name for theirs!

On a pedantic note, I use the term 'disorder' where this is the generally accepted name for a condition, or the terminology within that field. I am aware that there are negative connotations with the idea of 'disorder' and that the term is not favoured by all. In my professional practice, I use the term 'condition', but here I go with whatever is widely known and accepted for ease. I have also mainly stuck with accepted medical diagnostic criteria, wherever defined, despite there being some debate over the suitability of some of these criteria to define certain conditions accurately and in a way that represents real presentation. The purpose of the book is for initial guidance of characteristics. Further reading should be undertaken to gain a more in-depth understanding of the presentation of any of these conditions.

This book is not a replacement for diagnosis or assessment by a qualified professional person, or indeed a diagnostic tool in itself, but a reference point for clarifying suspicions and some guidance in what to do next.

Finally, it must be acknowledged that we owe so much to neuro-diverse individuals over history who have made discoveries and advancements possible. If these people had been average thinkers, more concerned with socializing and going along with everyone else, the world would be a poorer place. Mozart, Einstein and numerous others are all mooted to have been eccentric, single-focused individuals with unusual habits and perhaps affected by some form of neuro-diversity. Lists of present-day celebrities and thinkers with these conditions can be found on the Internet – some verified, some only postulated. The genius, the mad professor and the geek are all likely to be on this spectrum. Embrace the odd, for they shall shape the universe!

CHAPTER 1

Defining Neuro-diversity

The term 'neuro-diversity' was first used by Harvey Blume in an article in The Atlantic (1998), where he said:

> Neuro-diversity may be every bit as crucial for the human race as biodiversity is for life in general. Who can say what form of wiring will prove best at any given moment? Cybernetics and computer culture, for example, may favor a somewhat autistic cast of mind. (Blume 1998)

The term is used to define a way of processing information and making sense of the world in a way that differs from the typical – sometimes called 'neuro-typical'. 'Neuro' refers to brain, so neuro-diverse means simply 'brain different'. There is no conclusive list of which conditions should be included under the neuro-diverse banner and so there may be some surprises and some conditions which the reader might have expected to find which have been left out.

The information that is processed differently can come in any form: visual, verbal, auditory, tactile or as motor coordination or balance. This information needs to be sorted, stored and made available for recall by the brain when required. Those with neuro-diverse conditions can have difficulties carrying out any or all of these processes, or be extraordinarily good at them – such as having exceptional memory and recall, or having poor focus and attention ability.

The profile of such an individual can be what is sometimes known as 'spiky', in that they can be extremely accomplished at certain tasks – beyond that of a neuro-typical person – and yet unable to do other things, which may be generally perceived to be at a lower complexity level, a more 'simple' task. There appears to be no correlation between intellectual intelligence and what the person can or cannot do well. A person with Asperger syndrome, for example, may be able to study to advanced degree level and yet not be able to operate a kettle or a microwave, or a person with dyslexia may have a highly creative mind that finds multiple solutions to problems and yet get lost making a short journey that they have made several times before.

The one consistent thing about any person with any of these types of diversity is their inconsistency. Every person is different. Even if their diagnosis says the same condition, the way they are affected and the behaviours they present will be markedly different. This is important to note when it comes to discussing strategies and approaches for supporting people. There is no general one size fits all method that will deal with everyone with that condition. Support needs to be tailor-made and individualized. People with neuro-diversity are as varied as people who aren't, perhaps even more so.

Causes

For most of the conditions in this book, conclusive evidence is not available as to any one specific cause. It is more likely that a number of factors exists that may increase the likelihood of someone developing in this way. There are certainly strong familial links for many neuro-diverse conditions, where other members of the person's family also experience similar characteristics. A number of genes have been identified which seem to point to a predisposition to certain conditions and means of information processing. Current research suggests an immaturity in certain cells in the brain which create connections and pathways. The prefrontal and frontal lobe areas of the brain seem to be implicated as these are the areas which permit attention, memory and emotions. It is the part which processes information from the limbic system – our 'dinosaur', primitive, fight or flight brain – and modifies these reactions to make them socially acceptable. This is a very simplified version of events within the brain and there is far more than just this going on, but there are better people to explain that in other texts. This makes sense when we consider the characteristics of many neuro-diverse conditions, which often exhibit differences in social behaviour, social understanding, short-term memory and in monitoring, interpreting and expressing emotions.

So, on the whole these are lifelong, probably genetic, neurological conditions. They do not appear suddenly, unless there has been some kind of brain injury or damage (and which applies only to certain conditions), which can result in characteristics very similar to these conditions. They cannot be caught from anyone and they are unlikely to disappear, although their manifestations may change over the lifespan dependent mostly on external factors and how someone can manage their life to minimize the difficulties and maximize the strengths.

There is an alternative perspective when looking at neuro-diversity, which often originates from the community of individuals affected. This subscribes to the idea that this type of difference is a social construct and only a 'disability' in the way it deviates from social norms. Due to the lack of medical tests which provide a categorical diagnosis, neuro-diversity may be seen by some as a broad spectrum of behaviours, many of which are experienced by the general population, becoming a 'problem' only when they reach the extreme ends and where they conflict with the majority view of society as a whole. Thus, it could be suggested that these conditions don't exist as entities separate from the general population, but are merely variations of normal human behaviour with no definitive cut-off point between 'normal' and 'disabled'.

Co-morbidity

The first thing to note about these types of conditions is that they tend not to occur in isolation; that is, if you have one, it seems that you may be more likely to experience one or more others. As I heard Lorna Wing, one of the most eminent figures in autism, say (at a conference in Denmark in 2009) when discussing the overlapping of conditions in almost all individuals with autism: 'Nature doesn't draw a line without smudging it'. Her point was that there is no definitive cut-off and delineation where one condition stops and another starts; they often all merge into one another and each does not fit perfectly into any one set of diagnostic criteria. Human beings are far too individual and complex for that. Lorna Wing and her colleague, Judith Gould, also said that when diagnosing autism, the clinician should not stop there, but ask: 'What else?' I would suggest that this applies to the entire neuro-diverse spectrum. Hence, someone with dyslexia may also have characteristics of social anxiety, dyspraxia, obsessive-compulsive disorder (OCD) and maybe a dash of ADHD thrown in for good measure and thus they may not clearly fit into one of the preordained categories that we would like to put them to determine what we should do with them next. The brain is a complex mechanism and differences in its neurological development and processing do not fit neatly into boxes, thereby making simple, objective diagnosis of an individual easy and possible. Everyone's brain operates in a slightly different way to everyone else's and the assessment and diagnosis of developmental conditions is (currently) largely a subjective business and should be carried out with the intention of identifying the individual profile of abilities and weaknesses of the person to enable them to obtain the support and treatment they require, even if they don't neatly sit where we would like them to for funding or statistical purposes. Sadly, that is not generally how the system works.

Diagnosis

Each of the conditions included in this book has a set of criteria by which the characteristics can be identified. If a person is assessed as meeting these criteria and that this is not because of some other condition, disability or illness, a positive diagnosis should be given. Even so, some of the diagnostic criteria are often thought to be somewhat vague and not representative of the true nature of the condition, particularly as experienced by adults.

This book contains many mentions of the DSM-IV (*Diagnostic and Statistical Manual of Mental Disorders*, version IV: American Psychiatric Association (APA) 1994). This is the US classification system, which is widely recognized worldwide as the main source of information on criteria for neurological and psychological conditions. It may not be the most accurate source for a true representation of the characteristics and is sometimes criticized as such, but for consistency, this has been the text from which the diagnostic criteria for individual conditions are summarized. A similar classification system is more commonly used in the UK and Europe; the World Health Organization's (1994) *International Classification of Diseases*, known as the ICD-10. Both of these manuals are due for revision in the coming years and changes may be made to criteria and the names of some of the conditions featured in this book.

The variety of characteristics can make them difficult to crow-bar into one set of criteria. For the diagnostician, the nature of neuro-diversity can make it difficult to pin down which cocktail of conditions a person has and how they affect them. The process of diagnosis is different for different conditions, for example, Asperger syndrome, as a medical condition, needs to be diagnosed by a clinically qualified practitioner, such as a clinical psychologist or psychiatrist, whereas Tourette syndrome and anxiety disorders can be diagnosed by a general practitioner (GP), preferably one with extensive experience. Dyslexia is often seen as a learning difficulty (not to be confused with learning disability, which officially denotes an IQ level of 70 or below), it is most likely to be identified within an educational context and so an educational psychologist is the most likely assessor. The judgement and procedure as to who can perform the assessment or diagnosis may vary from country to country and so information should be sought locally as to who is the correct practitioner to carry this out.

A diagnostician will usually make their assessment based on observation, tests and interviews, but this will be a subjective judgement as there are currently no definitive, clinical tests which determine 100 per cent that a person is affected by any of these developmental conditions. Obviously, the level of their clinical experience can play a big part in identifying a correct diagnosis. Some adults report a lack of trust in the expertise of those carrying out diagnoses for neuro-diverse conditions, as due to their general, broad training, they may have little knowledge or experience of specific conditions. Tales of misdiagnosis, missed diagnosis and refusal to diagnose are many and varied within the adult neuro-diverse population. Let's hope that with ever increasing understanding, incidences of these will reduce.

The assessment may also be carried out by someone who has never met the individual before. The nature of neuro-diversity can be that characteristics appear or disappear in certain situations and therefore a true representation of the extent of the condition may not be seen on the day of the assessment, for whatever reason. For those who require additional support, accommodation or state benefits, a full diagnosis or formal assessment may be necessary.

It should, in fact, be easy to diagnose adults as they are often able to articulate their difficulties and characteristics and have perhaps researched to identify their own condition. They then may just require confirmation of what they already know through a diagnostician. My experience of carrying out informal assessments on adults who think they may have Asperger syndrome is that they are invariably right. Someone doesn't get as far as seeking out and possible paying for an assessment if they haven't already ruled out almost every other possible cause.

Alongside medically or educationally qualified diagnosticians (either funded or private), there are organizations and individuals offering private assessments, some of which may not hold the same weight as a clinical diagnosis. This may be a cheaper alternative and may be sufficient for the person's purpose. This can provide confirmation, further understanding and sometimes a letter of recommendation for full diagnosis to a medical or educational diagnostician, but may not allow access to disability benefits, medical insurance or other support services. It is important to clarify exactly what is being paid for and who is carrying out the assessment or diagnosis when seeking private services.

For some adults, self-diagnosis is enough. The limited access to funded diagnosis, high cost of private assessment or diagnosis and subjectivity of an 'official' diagnosis carried out by an unknown practitioner mean that some decide that their own knowing is all they need. Reading and researching the condition and meeting others who share the same life experience can be very helpful in confirming these initial suspicions.

To follow the funded assessment or diagnosis route, a sympathetic and understanding GP or psychologist is required to make an appropriate referral or diagnosis – depending on the conditions. There are reports of some professionals being unaware of these conditions and refusing to concede that this may be a possibility. There may also be long waiting lists for diagnosis or assessment in some areas and a lack of experience of working with adults for some diagnosticians, which can result in an unexpected diagnosis, which the individual may feel is incorrect. Before seeking diagnosis, it is useful to ask oneself:

- I am sure that I have this condition, but what will I do if the clinician says that I do not?
- Will I seek a second opinion (which may also concur with the first)?
- Will I have to start again with my search for who I am?
- Will I ignore the diagnosis and remain firm in my belief that I have this?

It is also worth considering what the benefits of an official diagnosis may be:

- access to services – housing, social care, etc. – where these exist
- access to welfare benefits on the grounds of disability or incapacity
- access to educational support – equipment, concessions and additional tutor time
- being taken seriously by family, friends and professionals
- having one's own suspicions 'officially' verified.

This decision is a personal one and should be considered carefully, perhaps in discussion with others and doing some research on what the options and services will be available in the local area, as this can vary greatly. Improvements in availability and consistency in funded adult diagnostic services is badly needed to ensure that individuals have faith in the diagnosis that they receive and also that they are guaranteed some follow-up support after it is made.

After the diagnosis, there is often the natural expectation that some ongoing support will follow. Unfortunately, this is often not the case as adult, specialist neuro-diversity support is few and far between. The most prolific source of information is the Internet with numerous resources, groups and forums with individuals, family members and professionals learning about themselves and each other. There are some funded services, but these are financially stretched and may have waiting lists. There is some private provision in the form of counselling or coaching support, but these can be costly.

Reaction to diagnosis or self-diagnosis

The overwhelming reaction for the majority of people I have met, who have been diagnosed or self-diagnosed in adulthood, has been one of relief: 'it wasn't my fault'. To have an explanation for all of the missed opportunities, the social faux pas, the anxiety and frustration, is hugely valuable to many people. There may be a grieving period where the person has to come to terms with the fact that things are not going to change radically and that they may always experience some difficulties in certain situations, but beyond that, for most people, is relief. Some describe a weight lifting from their shoulders and their life experiences suddenly make sense. As they trawl through their memories of failed jobs, difficult relationships, times of stress and confusion, it all starts to become clear as to what was really going on. Then, from that point, there is often a period of more learning about the condition; reading, speaking to others and getting a sense of 'who I am' with this new understanding. It can take some time, sometimes years, to fully redefine oneself as a person with a condition. The final stage for some is that this discovery is not an excuse to give up or behave how one chooses, but an opportunity to identify the areas in which support may be required and communicate these needs to others. It is also often necessary to learn new ways to manage situations and find new ways to navigate relationships to ensure that all parties can get their needs met.

This initial relief is not always shared by those who are part of the person's life. As far as they are concerned, the person with the condition is still the same as they have always been and any problems that were there before still remain. The grieving period for partners and family members may be longer and greater as they realize that the person is unlikely to be able to change. For some, the sense of hope feels dashed; they had always hoped that if things went right or they tried hard enough, their partner or family member might just become 'normal'. A diagnosis can provide the confirmation that this is not likely to happen.

Learning about the condition and seeking appropriate support or counselling can be beneficial for family members who struggle with this. It is important to find someone who has some level of understanding of the condition, so that they do not mistakenly judge the behaviour of the person. With time and support, many partners and family members do come to terms with viewing their loved ones in a different way.

It is useful to remember that the person themselves hasn't changed, it's just that now the 'instruction manual' for their effective operation is available: we now know why they do what they do and we know that it isn't a deliberate attempt to be difficult or awkward. They simply have a different understanding and way of processing information. This is invaluable information and should allow huge improvements to be made in communication and relationships. By providing a low stress environment for the person with neuro-diversity, their strengths and ability to be supportive is increased. By communicating in certain ways, confusion and misunderstanding are reduced. By having a good understanding of the strengths and limitations of someone with neuro-diversity, responsibilities can be shared to allow each person to do what they're best at. Understanding that the person is doing their best, even though it might not always look that way is crucial for all neuro-diverse relationships.

CHAPTER 2

Adult Attention Deficit Hyperactivity Disorder/Attention Deficit Disorder (ADHD/ADD)

It's hard for me to imagine what life would be like if I didn't have Adult ADHD. I don't know any different; I have always been like this. If I didn't have it, I don't know who I would be. It is such a huge thing and it affects every single thing I do and who I am: how I eat, how I shop, my moods, the way I do things.

Introduction

The first thing that often confuses people about ADHD/ADD is the name. Are ADHD and ADD the same thing? The answer will depend on who you ask. There are those who believe that ADD (attention deficit disorder) is ADHD without the hyperactivity element and that this constitutes a different condition, and there are those who routinely interchange ADD for ADHD. We'll go with the latter for the main reason that the *Diagnostic and Statistical Manual of*

Mental Disorders (DSM-IV: APA 1994) uses the term ADHD for its criteria and that gives some consistency with the other conditions covered in this book. ADD was the previous known term diagnostically and so has now been replaced by ADHD in standard usage. Adult ADHD is defined as a condition distinct from ADHD by some of those who have it, because the features are different due to the developmental age and level of those affected. That is acknowledged here, but will not be specifically used in this chapter.

The next thing which has been the subject of some controversy is whether ADHD actually exists. There are some who suggest that it is a neurological condition, affecting the frontal lobe area, and others who say that evidence for this being the case is scarce and that this collection of characteristics do not make up a disorder or condition, but are just a set of typical human behaviours or the result of poor parenting, bad diet and a range of other causes. No doubt this debate will rage on for a while yet. For our purposes and for the benefit of those living with a diagnosis of ADHD, we'll assume it does exist and is likely caused by biological or neurological factors, rather than solely environmental ones.

ADHD is characterized by an inability to inhibit or control impulses, which lead to a lack of focus and attention, restlessness and emotional reactions (rather than thought). We may be used to the idea of hyperactive, impulsive and out of control children affected by this condition, but what happens when they grow up? Most people move beyond tantrums and running around the place as they get older, but the characteristics can still have a considerable impact on an adult. The adult with ADHD may find that they cannot settle down and finish a task, find planning and organizing themselves difficult or perhaps feels that their brain is running on hyper-speed all the time and they cannot switch off. The benefits of ADHD can result in a person who can manage several different jobs or projects at the same time, is highly creative and motivated and will dive headlong into new adventures and ideas.

History

Although the name ADHD has been around only since the 1980s and it is commonly considered to be a newly discovered condition, similar characteristics have been observed for quite some time. It is widely claimed that the characteristics of what we now know as ADHD were first discussed by Dr Heinrich Hoffman in 1845 in a children's story about a character called 'Fidgety Phillip', although Dr Alexander Crichton reported a 'mental restlessness' and a 'disease of attention' in his book on mental derangement (1798, p.271, cited in Palmer and Finger 2001). A century later, a British paediatrician, Sir George Still, gave a series of lectures describing some children he had observed who he portrayed as lacking in attention, overly active and defiant. He claimed that their behaviour was either the result of brain injury around the time of birth or inherited, but not the result of poor parenting. Other definitions such as 'minimal brain damage' and 'hyperactivity' have been used over the years to describe these same characteristics. Changes to the Diagnostic Statistical manual (DSM) criteria over the years, resulting from increased knowledge and understanding, have attempted to clarify the situation regarding the different subtypes of ADHD. It was the belief that ADHD was, for the majority, a childhood condition, which disappeared around adolescence. This has now been demonstrated not to be the case, with many adults continuing to be affected by these behaviours.

Causes and current thinking

ADHD has been and continues to be the subject of considerable debate as to its nature, existence and cause. Opinions vary widely as to all of these. There are those who feel that ADHD is no more than simply a range of behaviours experienced in differing degrees by everyone – that some people are just more attentive, less impulsive and more able to follow instructions than others. There are concerns, particularly among child diagnoses, that the label is sometimes applied to children who demonstrate characteristics no different than those seen in most children at various times.

There is currently no conclusive evidence as to the cause of ADHD, although it is widely suspected to have some biological basis, with levels of brain chemicals being affected. Differing levels of dopamine, a neurotransmitter which affects the ability to maintain attention, as well as affecting other functions, are thought to play a part. Genetic and environmental factors are also being researched as possible causes. ADHD is thought to run in families and therefore may have some inherited or genetic link. Similarly to autism and Asperger syndrome, the frontal lobe area of the brain has been implicated, which affects the ability to problem solve and inhibit impulses.

The focus of much of the debate around ADHD has been on children, with medication, such as Ritalin, being both lauded and condemned in equal parts. ADHD was largely thought to diminish or disappear around adolescence, but increasing reports from adults refute this. Estimates as to the prevalence of Adult ADHD vary wildly, but it is largely thought that many of these adults remain undiagnosed – or wrongly diagnosed – and unaware that their behaviour may have a cause and a name. A figure of 15 per cent is estimated as the number of those diagnosed in childhood still having a full range of characteristics at the age of 25, with 65 per cent experiencing enough characteristics to impact on their daily lives (National Health Service (NHS) 2008). It is not yet clear whether ADHD can exist in adults without it appearing in childhood (the DSM-IV criteria require it to have an onset before seven years of age).

Diagnosis and assessment

The DSM-IV (APA 1994) criteria are specific in their requirements for diagnosis, including its maximum age of onset and the level of impairment that it must cause to warrant a diagnosis. These criteria are considered incomplete by some and are generally focused on child behaviour, rather than that of adults. Applying the childhood characteristics to adults is not an accurate way of diagnosis due to developmental changes that naturally take place during maturity; also the coping strategies created may mask the true extent of the disability. As with many psychological conditions, diagnosis is difficult due to the nature of overlapping or co-morbid conditions and the lack of a definitive test. It is also not always easy to identify the level of impairment caused by a spectrum of behaviours, many of which may be seen in the general population to a lesser or greater degree. ADHD is commonly dealt with by mental health professionals and diagnosed by a clinical psychiatrist. It is a complex and much misunderstood condition, which should be diagnosed only by an experienced practitioner. The diagnosis should include a full medical and developmental history tracing the characteristics back to early childhood (as required by the current diagnostic criteria). Family members and school reports may be used to provide more information on childhood history.

The DSM-IV criteria and guidelines are summarized here (APA 1994). In their original form they refer to child behaviours and have been slightly generalized here to make them more relevant to adults. The revised DSM-V, due for publication in 2012, may review these criteria and they may have some changes. Further examples of how ADHD may show itself in adults are outlined in the next section of this chapter.

To meet the DSM-IV criteria, the symptoms must occur in multiple settings and cause significant impairment in the individual's ability to function, thus it will differ considerably from similar behaviours as exhibited in the general population. Some of the symptoms must have been present prior to 7 years of age and they must cause significant impairment in more than one setting. They should also not be better classified as another disorder (such as an anxiety or mood disorder) nor must they only occur as part of another diagnosable disorder (such as a psychotic disorder or pervasive developmental disorder).

Three types of ADHD are identified with each requiring a different set of specified criteria to be met (list A and/or list B), with at least six symptoms to be met to a degree which disrupts normal functioning or development. These are as follows:

- ADHD – combined type: combined type ADHD requires both criteria from list A and list B to be met for more than six months.

- ADHD – predominantly inattentive type: this type requires only criteria from list A to be met for more than six months.

- ADHD – predominantly hyperactive-impulsive type: this type requires only criteria from list B to be met for more than six months.

Summary of list A symptoms, which denote inattention difficulties:

- difficulty maintaining attention on tasks

- appears not to listen to verbal instructions

- difficulty paying attention to detail – makes errors in tasks or activities

- fails to complete required tasks

- difficulty organizing self and activities

- hard to concentrate for long periods of time

- easily distracted, appears to procrastinate
- disorganized – loses possessions
- generally forgetful.

Summary of list B symptoms, which denote hyperactive and impulsive behaviours:

- fidgeting and restless behaviour
- difficulty in remaining still when required to
- excessive talking
- very active and always doing something
- difficulty waiting for own turn
- interrupts in conversation or activities
- difficulty inhibiting impulse to speak before required.

For those who have initial suspicions that they or another adult may have traits of ADHD, there is the Jasper/Goldberg Adult ADD Screening Examination – Version 5.0, which is available at various locations online (e.g. Jasper and Goldberg 1993; see also Resources). The test asks 24 questions relating to ADHD characteristics. A score above 70 may indicate ADHD and warrant further investigation. This test is not a diagnosis, but an indication of the presence of this type of behaviour.

Once diagnosed, there is very little specialist support for adults with ADHD and the person may find that they have to manage on their own.

Characteristics

ADHD can be very obvious in an adult, but this is not always the case. General opinion is that the main aspect of ADHD is disinhibition, which results in an inability to control one's own behaviour and impulses and stop one's self from reacting to situations without thought. Although the condition is experienced differently by each individual, the foremost visible traits are likely to be a person who seems unable to see things through to their natural conclusion, who may be easily distracted and often moving on to new things while midway through something else. For some people, a restlessness and boundless energy can be seen, sometimes combined with very rapid speech, which gives a sense of the person's brain moving too quickly for them to get their words out quick enough. The ADHD adult can come across as a chaotic, but exciting person, who is quite disorganized and loses things regularly. It is important to note that these characteristics have to be observed over various settings and not just when a person may be expected to be excitable or distracted. They must also be experienced to a degree which causes an impact on the person's ability to manage daily life, rather than just a variation of normal behaviour.

The following are a number of characteristics that may be observed in an adult with ADHD:

- procrastination – seems unable to begin a task
- quick tempered and easily irritated
- able to manage multiple jobs/roles/tasks at one time
- doesn't finish things before starting new ones
- may have many creative ideas
- has boundless energy and enthusiasm
- forgetful and often losing things
- speaks very rapidly and sometimes very loudly
- always moving their body – unable to be still
- unable to maintain focus and attention

- interrupts people with own ideas – poor listener
- may be a risk-taker with limited perception of danger
- very impatient – has to do everything 'now'
- hard to consider another's perspective over one's own immediate desires
- spontaneous
- adventurous – will have a go at anything
- careless and pays little attention to detail – speed over quality
- quick-witted and often humorous
- charismatic, exciting personality.

Implications

There is little research into the effects of ADHD on adults, but incidences of mental health issues and difficulties maintaining social relationships are all reported. Co-morbidity is said to be the rule, rather than the exception (Searight, Burke and Rottnek 2000) with substance misuse, depression, bipolar disorder and generalized anxiety disorder all sharing common features with ADHD. It is not clear if these conditions are experienced as a result of trying to cope with ADHD or whether they are just associated with it.

Alcohol or drug use may be a form of self-medication, where a person tries to calm their overactive brain with the substance, which enables them to concentrate and see a task through to completion; something which they may find impossible unaided. This often leads to problems of its own as a reliance and/or addiction to the substance used can cause increased anxiety and ill health (Tinsley and Hendrickx 2008).

Depression and anxiety are often the result of feeling different or unable to participate in the same activities as other people. This can lead to social isolation and exclusion, which further exacerbates depressed and anxious feelings.

In personal relationships, the person with ADHD can be initially excited by a new partner and experiences, but find it difficult to maintain interest after the 'honeymoon' period is over and the relationship becomes more mundane and routine. The ADHD partner may forget events and issues that are important to their partner and appear to be uncaring. Practical daily tasks may pile up due to procrastination and lack of ability to organize oneself. On a more positive note, an ADHD partner is likely to be fun, exciting and never dull. They may be very attentive and affectionate and keen to meet their partner's needs.

In employment, ADHD can be both a benefit and a hindrance. In the right job role, it can bring flexibility, imagination, creativity and endless enthusiasm, which are all highly valuable skills. The downside can be that more boring tasks cannot be attended to with enough attention to detail, social skills can be a problem and organization can lead to inefficiency.

Treatments and approaches

Medication is widely accepted as an effective treatment for some aspects of ADHD. Ritalin and Dexedrine are reported to decrease inattention, reduce impulsivity and improve concentration for some people with ADHD, but not all. There are a number of other prescribed medications available, which should be discussed with a medical practitioner. Clinical guidelines from the National Institute for Health and Clinical Excellence (NICE 2008) state that medication should be part of a package of treatment, which addresses all aspects of a person's ADHD.

Counselling and cognitive behavioural techniques can be

beneficial in helping to come to terms with past difficulties with relationships and perceived failures and also in learning new techniques to deal with situations. Seeing a therapist with experience of ADHD in adults would be recommended.

Self-help approaches, some of which are outlined below, can be helpful for those who do not wish to take medication, or alongside their medication. Self-awareness and acceptance can reduce stress and attempts to be 'normal' by learning to live with and relish one's different skills and abilities.

Self-help strategies

- Learn all you can about ADHD. Read, speak to others and become educated. Self-awareness is important, as is educating those around you.

- Find a buddy, a mentor or a coach who will support you to maintain appropriate social behaviour, if this is needed. This should be someone whose judgement you trust and that you are willing to listen to.

- Exercise can have a positive effect on burning up excess energy. Put all that energy to good use and take up sport, do-it-yourself (DIY) projects or gardening. There are likely to be many voluntary organizations that could use someone with energy. Your local volunteer centre will have lists of all available opportunities.

- Good dietary habits may have an impact on some aspects of ADHD. High sugar, caffeine and alcohol consumption may exacerbate hyperactivity and inattention problems.

- Manage your stress levels. Some people with ADHD find stress very hard to deal with. Learn techniques to keep stress low and recognize the signs of increasing stress or anxiety.

- As well as learning stress management techniques, try to manage your whole life in ways which minimize stressful events and occurrences. Obviously, this is not possible 100 per cent of the time, but simple measures can make a difference.

- Learn to say 'No', or at least 'I'll get back to you', to avoid taking on too much and feeling overwhelmed.

- Learn listening skills and attendance at active listening training or social skills workshops. Observe other people and see how they speak to each other, slowly and without interruption; this can be a good way to learn social skills.

- Set up systems to help you organize your life. Use a diary, wall planner, calendar and/or work plan to help you to remember what needs to be done and when. Prioritize tasks to avoid feeling overwhelmed.

- Ask for help with deciding what needs to be done in what order, if this is hard to do. Other people can help you to prioritize.

- Do the things you are best at and enjoy most, first, so that you have enough energy to do them well – then you will be inspired to continue with the less interesting stuff.

- Recognize your strengths and attractive features – and praise them.

Supporting strategies

- Help the person to keep focused by encouraging them and reminding them of deadlines, while also appreciating how hard it is for them to focus for any length of time.

- Appreciate that life with ADHD can be exhausting and that burnout is very possible if a person takes on too much. Encourage rest and relaxation and enjoyable activities.

- Accept that the person with ADHD will always be like this to some extent and is not being deliberately difficult or impulsive.

- Take time out for yourself; supporting or living with someone with ADHD can be exhausting.

- Find your own support in partners' forums, friends and family, but be aware that many people do not understand ADHD and may feel that you are making excuses for the person.

Words from those affected

Allie, diagnosed with Adult ADHD, at the age of 37, describes her experience:

I was in the top class at school for both English and Maths, but I still left with only three O [Ordinary] levels. Mainly, I was just bored; I couldn't read the text books if I had no interest in them. When I was interested, it was easy. I went back and got more exams later in my life. When I told a work colleague that I was planning to study English A [Advanced] level at evening classes, she said: 'You'll never do it, you never see anything through'. I was determined to show her and even though I lost interest halfway through I kept going and got good marks.

I was diagnosed at the age of 37 after a friend suggested that I seemed to fit a list of characteristics of Adult ADHD. I went on the Internet, one of my obsessions, and looked it up. I had never considered that there was such a thing for how I was. It all fell into place. It was a mixture of relief that I was not 'naughty', 'difficult', 'lazy' or 'stubborn' as well as a great sadness and anger for all the wasted years when I had not known why I was like I was. I have accepted my Adult ADHD as a fact and I am not embarrassed to tell people that I have it; in fact, I am proud to be part of the Adult ADHD community. Initially, it felt like a bit of a stigma; having a name or a label took a bit of getting used to, especially as people don't understand what it is.

It's hard for me to imagine what life would be like if I didn't have Adult ADHD. I don't know any different; I have always been like this. If I didn't have it, I don't know who I would be. It is such a huge thing and it affects every single thing I do and who I am: how I eat, how I shop, my moods, the way I do things. I think I have become less confident since the diagnosis as I am more aware of how different I am to other people in the things I say and do and how I think. I cannot 'see' things that others 'get' without help. How do they know how to behave socially or what to say? I have no idea what is appropriate. A situation will arise and I will see it so differently to everyone else. I am so aware of that since finding out about my Adult ADHD. People say I am bonkers and a good laugh. I have a feeling that I might be very boring without my Adult ADHD. I think it helps me in my job as an IT trainer, where I have to stand up in front of people all day and keep them entertained.

The main characteristics of Adult ADHD for me are my impulsiveness, inability to control my emotions, inattention, forgetfulness and hyper-focus. I will just do things 'now' and yet if I'm going somewhere in the future, I need to plan down to the tiniest detail, so it feels like a contradiction. I have walked out of jobs and bought cars without thinking things through and yet on other occasions have to control every aspect of a decision by researching every detail obsessively and then being unable to make a decision.

I get bored very quickly and the concept of practice makes perfect does not work for me. If I practice, I get bored. I will jump into something new at the most difficult level straight away, which I find challenging and exciting. I can also never do the same thing twice; I would be bored and be unable to put in the required effort.

My hyper-focus is both a positive and negative thing for me. It can enable me to focus for hours and hours on end on one task or topic, but can also mean that I can become totally absorbed by something to the point of not being able to see anything else that might need doing instead. It can mean that I become hyper-focused on things which are not very useful, like the Internet. I am an all or nothing type of person, I have to have the time to focus on something 100 per cent and cannot just dip in and out of things for half an hour or so at a time. This can give me such determination that I will work hard at finding a solution to a problem when others would just give up. At other things, where my interest is not there, I will just give up straight away. I am on medication and this helps me to get a lot more done these days. I can clean my house from top to bottom and it will look amazing and then I notice that it has got all messy again. I don't understand how that happens, how it can go from one to the other. I can't keep things tidy as I go along; it's all or nothing. I have to wait until I can stand it no more and then put it right again.

My Adult ADHD makes me hard work in friendships and relationships. I know I am a demanding friend and I have very intense friendships with people. I can get very enthusiastic about something very minor and can focus on myself and own needs, which can make me appear selfish. I rely on my close friends for support and help. I need people to be very patient and accommodating to my difficulties. Life is very draining for me and also I am draining for others. There is never a dull moment in my life. I don't go out of my way to attract trouble, but things just seem to happen to me. It's like living on a rollercoaster and anyone who wants to share my life has to be prepared to live on one with me. I have found Adult ADHD forums incredible. To find all those other people just like you, that's great. Reading about other people having the same daily struggles helps me to realize that I'm not lazy; it's just how my brain works.

I find it hard to control my emotions; I get very angry, frustrated and sad very easily. I can't let go of things and get too emotionally involved. For example, when I see news stories about something happening to children or animals, I can't disassociate myself emotionally and I won't sleep for weeks, I'll cry and I can't seem to let it go; I just keep reliving the suffering over and over again.

I try to use strategies to help me manage my life, but I often find that I can't stick to them for long. I rely on my friends, who guide me when I need them and I am trying to use mindfulness techniques, but unfortunately this requires practice, which I am not good at. The biggest thing which has helped me is my awareness of Adult ADHD. I can recognize when my behaviour is due to my Adult ADHD and try to combat or control it.

CHAPTER 3

Autistic Spectrum Conditions

Asperger Syndrome, High Functioning Autism and Pervasive Developmental Disorder – Not Otherwise Specified (PDD-NOS)

I would never want to think differently, I enjoy functioning the way I do.

Introduction

Autism is perhaps the most complex condition covered in this book, with probably the most written about it; hence, it is the longest chapter. There is currently a great deal of interest in autism and Asperger syndrome, with the media fascinated by these individuals who can present a range of abilities and so-called disabilities, which can sometimes challenge all that we think we know about people, their behaviour and their motivation. Those on the autistic spectrum relate differently socially and often our assumptions about what is 'normal' social behaviour and desire are entirely misguided.

Adults with so-called higher functioning autistic conditions, such as Asperger syndrome, are typically intellectually able and yet have significant difficulties in relating to people and the social world. They may find friendships and personal relationships difficult to form, understand and maintain and be less able to 'read' unspoken social rules than other people. This can cause offence and exclusion, leading to problems with depression, anxiety and low self-esteem. Other issues for these people can include a low tolerance of change; they prefer to live a routine-led life which has little variety. Sensory issues have an impact for some people who find they experience the physical senses in a more or less heightened way to others, resulting in noise, physical touch, smell or other sensory perception being difficult to tolerate.

The autistic spectrum ranges across intellectual levels from those with a learning disability (Classic or Kanner's autism) to those without (high functioning autism, Asperger syndrome, PDD-NOS), but it should be noted that 'intelligence' is not a good indicator of ability or disability within autism as the profile of the person can be very variable from one skill to another. We are looking at those at the end of the spectrum which generally does not include a learning disability (high functioning autism, Asperger syndrome, PDD-NOS), rather than 'autism'.

History

The term 'autistic', coming from the Greek 'aut' meaning 'self' to describe different types of individuals presenting socially detached behaviours, has been used over the centuries, but case studies or examples are scarce and little is known of those described in this way. In the 1940s, both Leo Kanner and Hans Asperger discussed children they had worked with who had a puzzling profile of both amazing talents combined with sometimes profound learning disabilities (Frith 2008). Kanner was an American, writing in English, and his work has led to his identification of Kanner's autism, sometimes known as classic autism, which we currently define as autism disorder, meaning those who have a language delay or limited language and who have a high probability of having a learning disability (lower than average intelligence level). The work of Asperger, who wrote in German, was rediscovered and translated into English only in the 1980s. Asperger described a group of children who had average or above average, intelligence levels and yet displayed profiles very similar to those described by Kanner. He observed that these children had difficulties with interacting socially and making friends that was unusual given their general profile. He noted that the tone and rhythm of their speech was unusual and that they seemed to have difficulties relating emotionally, with a tendency to deal with emotions in a logical, intellectual manner. They also were seen to have narrow subjects of interest, which were all-absorbing and took their full attention for extended periods (Attwood 2006).

The term 'Asperger syndrome' was first used in the English-speaking world by Lorna Wing, one of the pioneers of modern-day autism research, who also placed it within the autistic spectrum. She developed the original 'triad of impairments' of autism, communication, imagination and social interaction, which she saw that Asperger syndrome fitted into. Asperger's original work was translated into English by Uta Frith in 1991 in the first major publication on the subject. Separate diagnostic criteria were added to the DSM in 1994 and since then interest and knowledge of this condition has grown. PDD-NOS developed as a category usually used to describe someone who has characteristics of Asperger syndrome, but to a lesser intensity or degree.

Causes and current thinking

Autistic spectrum conditions are neurological in origin with clear indications that different parts of the brain work in a different way than those of non-autistic people. As with many of the conditions in this book, the frontal lobe area, which controls social behaviour, emotions and impulses, is implicated. Synapses, which allow the transfer of information from cell to cell within the brain, are said to be weaker and less efficient in those on the autistic spectrum and other neuro-diverse conditions (Pauc 2008). A whole host of genes have been identified which appear to play a part in the development of autism and strong familial tendencies towards similar characteristics are seen (which puts paid to the idea that people on the autistic spectrum do not marry or have children!). Autism is experienced in a very individual way for each person with the condition and as such it may well be that a very individual profile of gene mutations and differences is seen in each person, rather than there being one genetic explanation for autism as a whole.

Professor Simon Baron-Cohen (2004) sees foetal testosterone levels as a player in the autism debate and there may be developments in foetal testing for autism in the future. This, of course, raises ethical issues of whether the option of terminating a potentially autistic child would be of benefit to anyone. Arguably, without autism we would be without many of our great thinkers, scientists and mathematicians, who may fit within the Asperger syndrome definition. There are many other research programmes looking for causal factors and early identifiers for autism and this work will be ongoing for many years to come.

It is thought that a number of factors may combine to create a greater likelihood of someone having autistic features and exactly what these are and to what extent they enhance this likelihood is unknown. It is likely that these will vary from person to person. There may be a number of different routes which result in the characteristics of autism, for example brain injury can create very similar characteristics in some people. Current thinking seems to be focused on expanding how we see autism into a much broader perspective of causes, behaviours, levels of affectedness and whole person profiles, rather than just trying to fit people into generic boxes of criteria, into which many people don't fit entirely.

Diagnosis and assessment

It is worth noting initially that there are currently likely to be many young people and adults who have Asperger syndrome (AS) but have no diagnosis and may be unaware that they are affected by the condition. Due to the relatively recent translation and inclusion of AS and PDD-NOS in the diagnostic manuals, anyone born earlier than the late 1970s could not have had a childhood diagnosis, which is when differences in behaviour are most likely to be identified.

There is currently no medical test which can provide a categorical diagnosis for any autistic spectrum condition. This means that diagnosis is a subjective business, relying on the knowledge, experience and judgement of the diagnostician. The process of diagnosis for an adult usually involves interviews, sometimes psychometric tests to measure levels of reasoning and spatial ability, interviews or questionnaires completed by family members (if possible) to determine the existence of the behaviours in childhood and sometimes some tests which measure certain characteristics.

The path to a funded diagnosis requires referral to an appropriately qualified diagnostician – typically a clinical psychologist or psychiatrist, who may be based at a local (or not so local) hospital or at a specialist mental health clinic. This person will be experienced in working with adults as there are some differences in diagnosing children and adults. There is a private route to a professional clinician if one has the funds to pay for the diagnosis. The cost is in the realms of £2000 (US$ 3200 in July 2009). Each diagnostician may have their own methods, but all should gather extensive information from a number of personal sources over a period of time before making a decision.

It should be noted that for some adults, obtaining an official diagnosis is not important. Once they feel that AS answers their questions about themselves, they are satisfied. To know themselves is all they need.

There is much ongoing debate about autism and where the cut-off points are between different conditions on the spectrum. This will no doubt continue for some time. High functioning autism, Asperger syndrome and PDD-NOS are generally considered to be conditions on the autistic spectrum at the so-called 'high functioning' end. This means that the person has an intellectual ability within the normally expected range and therefore will have more processing skills to make sense of the world and their place in it. This does not make these conditions a 'mild' form of autism. It may be that the quality of life for someone with Asperger syndrome is poorer than that of a person with a severe learning disability and autism due to their awareness of their own difference, which can lead to depression.

The difference between high functioning autism and Asperger syndrome is widely debated. No one seems entirely sure if they are the same thing or separate. Within the DSM-IV criteria (APA 1994), high functioning autism (HFA) comes under the autistic disorder category, while Asperger syndrome has its own category. This may change under the DSM-V due for publication in 2012. Within the autistic disorder criteria, there is a requirement for a language or communication impairment to be present for a positive diagnosis, so we can assume that those with HFA do have a language or communication impairment, whereas for Asperger syndrome, normal language development is specified as a requirement. The other difference that I have noted in my work, and asked others working in the field to comment upon, is that as a very general rule, those with HFA seem to be quite content to live a mainly solitary life, perhaps choosing not to have personal relationships. In contrast, the majority of people with AS that I have met would like to have a social network, albeit a small and manageable one, and do seek personal relationships.

A diagnosis of PDD-NOS is given when clear autistic features are present, but not to the extent or quantity for a full diagnosis of Asperger syndrome. Many people find this confusing and use the term Asperger syndrome when describing themselves to others to aid understanding. It may well be that this diagnosis is incorporated into AS or autistic disorder in the future.

Knowledge of how autism and Asperger syndrome affect adults is increasing, but until recent years has been poor, with most resources and research focusing on children. There is still a belief for some people that autism only affects children and somehow disappears in adulthood.

Understanding of adult autism and AS within the medical profession is limited in some areas, with misdiagnosis or a refusal to refer a person for diagnosis commonly reported anecdotally. Reasons such as 'You can't have Asperger syndrome because you are 50 and someone would have spotted it by now' or 'You are married and people with Asperger syndrome can't get married' have been reported to me personally as to why someone is wrong about their suspicions of possible AS. Both are wrong.

Diagnostic criteria for Asperger syndrome cover the following and use similar terminology (such as 'impairment'). In the next section, we will look at how these translate to the behaviour of a person. The criteria for HFA, which is included under autistic disorder in the DSM-IV, are broadly similar. PDD-NOS follows the same criteria, but expects not to see quite so many or not to such a significant degree. It should also be noted that these criteria generally identify child behaviour and do not have an adult modification, which may outline the behaviour of young people and adults more accurately.

Social interaction – at least two of the following must be seen:

- impairments in non-verbal communication such as facial expression, eye contact, body language
- lack of peer relationships
- lack of desire to share interest or enjoyment with others
- lack of understanding of two-way nature of social and emotional relationships – tendency to be self-focused.

Patterns of behaviour and interests that are routine based and restricted – at least one of the following must be seen:

- narrow subjects of interest that are enjoyed to an unusual intensity
- need to stick to set routines and schedules with little flexibility
- repetitive motor movements – waving hands, clicking fingers, twisting body
- focus on detail, rather than whole picture.

There are four additional prerequisites for a positive diagnosis of Asperger syndrome. These are as follows:

- The characteristics seen cause a significant impairment in the functioning of the person – either socially, occupationally or in other areas.
- There was no significant language delay in childhood.

- There was no significant cognitive developmental delay in childhood.

- The characteristics are not better explained by another pervasive developmental disorder, or by schizophrenia.

Characteristics

Asperger syndrome and its autistic cousins are lifelong developmental disorders that affect how someone interacts and relates socially. They can also affect language, communication, information processing and decoding of social information and other external sensory stimuli, such as detail, noise and physical touch. People with AS have difficulty in 'reading' non-verbal communication, such as facial expressions and body language, and may choose to have a routine-led life with as few changes and unpredictable events as possible. Some people have difficulties with language and may have limited or no speech. They can often have difficulties with understanding the point and the rules of social interaction and relationships, finding social chat and small talk pointless and complicated. Many people with AS remain undiagnosed into adulthood and despite their often significant skills and intelligence levels, many people are unemployed and lead solitary existences, finding friendships and relationships demanding.

AS is characterized diagnostically by three main areas of difference from expected norms of behaviour: social interaction, social communication and language, and social imagination. Environmental sensitivity, although not mentioned specifically in the various diagnostic criteria for AS/HFA, is often said to feature as a factor for the majority of those with these conditions.

Social interaction

Someone with AS may be affected in social situations by the following:

- being unable to read social cues, which others seem to intuitively 'know'

- appearing to be naive, tactless or stupid by saying or doing the 'wrong' thing socially

- having difficulty appreciating thoughts, feelings and opinions of other people as being potentially different to one's own

- failing to adhere to social rules, resulting in ridicule, aggression or exclusion.

Someone with AS may typically appear to be awkward in social situations, not picking up on unspoken 'rules'. They may behave in a socially inappropriate way and find it hard to understand why their behaviour has offended or bothered others. For example, someone might mention how much weight a colleague has put on recently or speak very loudly about a personal issue and not be able to consider that others may find sensitive topics uncomfortable – the person would be able to see the matter only from their own viewpoint.

Many adults have a history of mainly negative social experiences, including a high probability of bullying, and may have given up on friendships and relationships, choosing a solitary existence which feels easier to manage.

For those who do maintain friendships, these tend to be one-to-one interactions, rather than large groups, and the person often has quite a small social network compared to a non-AS person. Social interaction is largely exhausting for people with AS, who have to work hard to translate the confusing social rules, non-literal language and facial expressions of others. Considerable periods of solitude are necessary for many people with AS in order to recharge and retreat from the world of people.

Social communication and language

A person with AS is likely to have difficulty with the following aspects of communication:

- reading non-verbal signals, body language and facial expression

- understanding subtleties of humour, subtext and non-literal meanings of spoken language

- needing very precise instructions and not being overloaded with information

- failing to accurately communicate, resulting in misunderstanding, stress and exclusion.

A person with AS may find the language and emotions on the face difficult to 'read'. They may struggle to make eye contact, finding it pointless or overwhelming. Due to missing extensive amounts of non-verbal communication, their language may be very pedantic and literal, needing to get most of their information verbally, rather than visually as well, as other people can and so requiring language to be very precise. Meaning may not be understood when others are more ambiguous and flexible with their language usage. They may also require information to be presented to them in a detailed and exact way in order for it to be understood. If the understanding is not there, the person may be paralysed and have no idea what to do or how to react. This can lead to feelings of inadequacy, stupidity and low confidence. Thinking tends to be logical and decisions are based on rational thought rather than emotions or feelings.

Social imagination

The concept of social imagination difficulties can manifest in any of the following:

- needing their own routines and preferred ways of doing things

- having limited interests and conversational topics

- disliking change, variety, surprises and spontaneity

- having rigid thought patterns which find new concepts, planning, consequences and abstract thought difficult

- being unable to tolerate flexibility, leading to stress, anxiety and difficulties within social relationships, as the person may be seen as selfish and uncaring of others' needs

- using black-and-white thinking – seeing only one or two options to any situation, an all-or-nothing approach to life with a difficulty to perceive other options or degrees.

Managing unpredictable situations or changes to routines can be very stress provoking for someone with AS. Due to their reduced ability to understand all of the social interactions around them, the person may cling to safe, known situations and routines in order to maintain a sense of control and familiarity in a world which feels chaotic and illogical. This can result in a narrow focus in both thought and action where the individual is unable to consider other perspectives or behaviours outside that which is already known. The person may, for example, insist on eating the same food every day, sit in the same seat on the bus and become agitated when this is not possible; they may find it difficult to manage changes at work or home. The tendency towards black-and-white thinking may result in unrealistic choices and perspectives. For example, someone in a relationship may feel that the relationship must be perfect and that any disagreement is a sign that it is a failure and should be abandoned. If it's not perfect, it must be terrible is the thinking and the ability to consider the other positive aspects are less developed.

Environmental sensitivity

Although not mentioned in the diagnostic criteria for AS, it is widely accepted that many individuals across the autistic spectrum experience differences in how they perceive the sensory environment, being either under-sensitive or over-sensitive to a range of senses, in comparison to a person with autism. The person may experience the following:

- a limited range of tolerance for certain noises, smells, textures or physical touch

- a need or strong preference for certain noises, smells, textures and physical touch

- an inability to tolerate or do without certain stimuli, resulting in isolation and withdrawal from environmental stressors.

Environments which are too stressful may be avoided by the person with AS as the sensory input is just too overwhelming for them to manage. Some people find being held or touched by another person unbearably uncomfortable, which has a big impact on personal relationships. Some find certain noises, smells or textures of fabrics intolerable. For others their experience of the sensory world is excessively underdeveloped and they may need to seek stimulation in order to feel anything. These are people who will seek strong smells, may self-harm or wear many layers of clothes to feel the pressure on their bodies and may enjoy spinning or swinging their body to feel the sensations more intensely.

Implications

Anxiety, depression and stress are commonly experienced by those with AS as a result of trying to live in a social world which makes little or no sense. Isolation and social exclusion are common as the person finds it difficult to make friends and retain those friendships due to not knowing how to do so in the same way that others appear to naturally understand.

Employment and education can be very successful as plenty of people with AS have good intelligence levels and the ability to focus on subjects that interest them. Anecdotal reports suggest that many high level academics and scientists could fulfil the criteria for AS and yet remain undiagnosed as they have found a specialist niche in which to work where their skills are highly respected and prized and their social 'quirks' are overlooked. This is not the case for everyone with AS, some of whom struggle to find employment or complete their studies. This can be due, not to their abilities, but to the social and environmental demands of any workplace or educational institution (Hendrickx 2008). Travelling to work on public transport, making small talk with colleagues, living in communal student accommodation and managing daily independent life can be overwhelming for someone with AS and they may feel unable to continue.

Treatments and approaches

There is no treatment or cure for AS, or any autistic condition, and for most people with AS, this would not be a desirable option, as their profile gives them many abilities that non-AS people do not have. Medication is sometimes given for anxiety, stress or depression experienced by those with AS, but not for the condition itself. Cognitive behavioural therapy (CBT) is generally accepted to be a helpful form of counselling therapy as it focuses on changing thoughts and behaviour, rather than on exploring emotions, which people with AS often find troubling and difficult. The more logical CBT approach seems to fit the natural AS profile better. Any technique which encourages stress management and relief could be helpful for someone with AS.

For many adults, the relief of diagnosis and the knowledge of who they are and why life has gone the way it has is the main strategy in an improved future. Self-awareness and self-acceptance are crucial in raising self-esteem and confidence, which is often lacking due to the negative reactions of others. Acceptance and understanding from others is also essential in recognizing that the person with AS is doing their best and not being deliberately pedantic or awkward. It can be hard to comprehend that a high-achieving expert in their scientific field may find the concept of making tea for everyone in the office (or even operating the kettle) impossible to understand or remember. This is a very uneven profile of ability, which can astonish!

There are few specialist adult support services, but those that do exist provide things like supported accommodation for those who want to live independently, but may not be able to do so entirely alone, employment support and help finding work and completing applications forms, as well as social groups and befriending support.

Self-help strategies

- Educate yourself in Asperger syndrome – self-awareness is essential in living with AS.

- Become aware of your own needs – having time on your own away from people, being given clear instructions, etc. – and communicate these to others.

- Use diaries and planners to help with short-term memory issues.

- Take regular exercise and periods of relaxation to help with stress and anxiety.

- Ask for help if you need it – this is not a sign of weakness or failure.

- Ask a trusted friend or person for advice and guidance in social situations.

- Remember that many people find socializing very difficult, but they just hide it well.

- Join online forums or local social groups for adults with AS – sharing experiences can reduce feelings of isolation.

Supporting strategies

- Remember that the person is likely to have a history of bullying and negativity – give positive regard as much as possible.

- Offer support with planning and organization – maps, timetables, schedules – as the person will struggle to plan without visual support and structure.

- Notify changes in advance wherever possible, because unexpected changes cause high levels of stress and anxiety.

- Facilitate and maintain the individual's preferred routines if these reduce stress and do not limit growth and personal development.

- Recognize that the person may have limited personal or social boundaries – these need to be stated clearly to maintain low stress levels. Do not give negative feedback when these boundaries are overstepped as this will not be personal or deliberate.

- Provide detailed instructions for tasks, with step-by-step guidance.

- Allow the person time to process questions and have time to answer them. Do not expect 'on the spot' responses without thinking time.

- Be aware of the invisibility of AS: verbal and academic ability may not give a true indication of the level of difficulties experienced.

- Remember that if someone with AS is behaving in a way that you consider to be unusual, you should ask them why in a positive way. Your assumptions for their behaviour could be very wrong.

- Be direct with instructions and requirements. Do not wrap up the message with meaningless words. Keep it brief and clear.

Words from those affected

Matt, who was diagnosed with Asperger syndrome at 44 years of age, describes his perspective of life on the autistic spectrum:

I can't really imagine not having AS (part of the syndrome, I suppose). I love having a diagnosis which explains some of the things I am good at, some of the things I am hopeless at, and why the coexistence of these traits can be so problematic. People expect someone with a degree in languages, translation theory and linguistics to be able to use a rucksack, straps and all. When they see you struggle to put it on, the immediate perception is of someone either mucking about or deliberately being obtuse. It is a problem to picture the manipulation required and the changes it will bring about which cause such difficulty for those with an autistic spectrum disorder.

I would never want to think differently, I enjoy functioning the way I do. I take great pleasure in playing games with my memory or the feeling of intense excitement when something which is especially interesting to me is forthcoming. I appreciate help I receive from others who can explain some things which I find difficult, and accept that I may never be able to learn to do them well or at all. Patience and understanding are key in my opinion.

I have a great long-term memory, especially for dates both historic and those pertaining to my life, especially my childhood. I do find it hard to empathize; although I have learnt intellectually what is required, I rarely feel I understand what others are going through emotionally. I have almost no common sense and find it extremely hard to follow verbal instructions of any length. I need written support to be effective. I now watch films with the subtitle option turned on, as I am able to follow the plot much more effectively. I have had a string of intense interests throughout my life. I am very aware that the feeling I have for these is exactly what I had when a small child. It is an overwhelming excitement as of Christmas approaching. I have very black-and-white, all-or-nothing thinking, seeing things as either perfect or hopeless. I also tend to believe others have the same thoughts and opinions as I do, leading me to not impart information in the belief the person is already in possession of such information. I have learnt facial expressions to some extent, but am often hopelessly wrong at guessing what people are thinking or feeling.

I have a small circle of friends who I know, and who know me, very well. They understand and accept that I may have problems with certain aspects of my life and tend to make allowances. My partners have generally been women who have asked me out, as I never really do the asking myself (not being sure of the best way and also out of fear of rejection and of looking stupid). More recently I have found the perfect solution with the advent of dating websites. One knows that the people on them are actively looking for a partner, and it is straightforward to narrow down the potential candidates to those with whom one might find the most compatibility.

I studied languages at university and feel that rather than learning them as others did, I often relied on my memory to get me through. I chose to study them because my family and teachers thought that it would be a good idea. I had no strong urge myself, I simply followed the advice of those I judged to know better than myself. I got through the course with the support of a very sympathetic girlfriend. Although neither of us knew of AS (it was not known about in the early 1980s) she could see I often struggled in social situations and had trouble following verbal instructions, for example. I was also still living at home at this time, so I was not under the pressure of independent living or sharing with strangers.

I have always suffered terribly from anxiety and stress, from when I was a small child up until relatively recently. It is the fear of change and of the unknown, which are greatly magnified in those with AS, since they are far less adaptable and flexible. I often fear change as I will have to learn a whole new coping strategy to deal with a new situation. I have also been prone to depression, being aware of my limitations. I find that cognitive behavioural therapy has worked very well for me in dealing with my anxieties and fears. It is a straight-forward and logical way of constructing coping strategies which are adaptable to different problems. I make sure that I keep myself in as stress-free an environment as possible, and remove from it anything which might make me anxious. Even though it might seem to some that I am not living up to my potential, I know that in fact I am creating an environment for myself in which I can function quite happily, which is all that I require from life. No anxiety, no tension, none of the feelings which plagued me before I ever heard of AS.

Up until my diagnosis I had suffered from quite low self-esteem. I could never quite work out why I struggled so much in some areas of my life, yet excelled in others. I didn't con-sider myself unintelligent yet felt stupid when around other people. Since my diagnosis, I feel transformed. I understand myself so much better, and can appreciate why I do what I do, and why I am not so able in other areas. My mental health has improved beyond all recognition and I am much less judgemental about my abilities and what I think I ought to be able to do and what level of success I should achieve in my life. As a child I often excelled in reading and writing, usually being near the top of my class. I would spend much of my playtime either drawing or making models of Nelson's Column, which was one of my strong interests when aged about 6. Teachers seemed puzzled but just left me alone as I was no trouble and was obviously absorbed in what I was doing.

When in my teens I sang in a world famous school choir. This had many benefits. I could avoid the rough and tumble of the playground as we were allowed to spend break time in the music department, and we also had preferential treatment in gaining access to the building for rehearsal. Singing in the choir was probably the most important part of my teenage years. My oldest friends today are still largely those I sang with 30 or more years ago. I spent most evenings in my teenage years on my own in my bedroom listening to recordings of some of the pieces I had learnt. I found it very soothing and the familiarity of the pieces never palled.

I have become adept at covering up the most obvious problems I have with AS. I avoid where I can situations where I might become anxious or stressed, I work part-time in an environment which for me is very familiar, a bookshop. I have always worked in different bookshops, finding it a comfortable and safe atmosphere to interact with the public. I am usually comfortable in dealing with queries and love the idea of selling knowledge, which books are.

CHAPTER 4

Dyslexia

By Claire Salter

I speak really quickly because it's hard for my mouth to keep up with my brain. My friends have got used to me now but when I meet new people I see them get lost during conversations with me.

Introduction

Among the neuro-diverse conditions described in this book, dyslexia is probably the most well known but perhaps the least understood. Although most people have heard of it, few could accurately describe the skill areas that dyslexia affects. While some stick to the oldest definitions (see History section later in this chapter) others argue that it doesn't even exist and is the result of poor schooling or a deprived background.

As the DSM-IV (APA 1994) recognizes the existence of dyslexia, arguments about its reality can be put to one side. However, a great deal of debate remains about its precise roots or causes and which characteristics can be ascribed to these. Even its very basis is subject to question with researchers looking at, variously, sensory, biological, neurological and a number of other bases.

There is much debate and disagreement about dyslexia, even in the terminology used to describe the syndrome. It has been known by a number of terms over time including 'word blindness', dyslexia, a specific learning difficulty (SpLD) and, more recently, a neuro-diversity. The term dyslexia has no intrinsic meaning in itself but is an umbrella term defining a spectrum of difficulties. There is no definitive definition but a variety of descriptions, which often appear contradictory. However, they do not necessarily negate each other but demonstrate how complex and wide ranging dyslexia is.

The term dyslexia comes from the Greek 'dys' meaning 'difficulty with' and 'lexia' meaning words or language. The syndrome of dyslexia is complex and subtle and eludes easy definition. There are manifold expressions of the syndrome and descriptions of its effects. Although divergent in many areas, there are some common agreements among researchers. For example, all current definitions of dyslexia centre upon deficits in short-term working memory, which affect people's ability to process information. In particular it is agreed that people with dyslexia may have difficulties receiving, holding, storing and retrieving information, especially if it is presented to them in speech or writing. (Department for Education and Skills 2004)

Despite each person having an individual profile of strengths and weaknesses, there is a common core and a pattern of thinking that can be seen as a cognitive style (Morgan and Klein 2000). As a result of their processing difficulties (or differences), people with dyslexia have an individual profile of strengths and areas of weakness and their difficulties will impact on them in a variety of ways. It is very important to identify and recognize strengths as well as areas needing support, then with the development of effective strategies, people with dyslexia can achieve their full potential.

In addition they may possess skills and abilities beyond those without such a 'disability'. However, without adequate and appropriate support and the development of strategies, people with dyslexia face the same difficulties throughout their life. In fact the difficulties they face may have a greater impact in adulthood than earlier on. A useful summary may be to say that dyslexia is a learning difficulty that causes problems with learning language-based skills in particular. Dyslexia can also affect concentration, short-term memory, maths, fine motor and communication skills. Being dyslexic is not a reflection of intelligence, it is about the ability to access intelligence. It is a neurological condition, which can make learning challenging.

History

The syndrome recognizable as dyslexia was described in 1896 in the case of Percy, a 14-year-old boy who couldn't learn to read despite not having difficulty with other tasks (Hinshelwood 1917). This case cemented the use of the term 'word blindness' misapplied to this day. At the start of the twentieth century a Scottish eye surgeon called James Hinshelwood described the congenital nature of these reading difficulties and tried to find their biological causes (Hinshelwood 1917, cited in Thompson and Watkins 1996). His work advanced the study of developmental dyslexia, evolving from identification and description to analysis and discussion of the syndrome and its components. It can be seen that from very early on, there was an understanding that dyslexia is a difficulty in specific skill areas not related to intelligence or opportunity and despite instruction.

In spite of this early recognition and ongoing research, dyslexia was largely ignored in the UK by the establishment until the 1970s when a report on special educational needs was written and dyslexia was included. Research around the world was more developed; for example, organizations in the USA noted that it encompassed a wider range of difficulties other than simply with reading and writing. As a result, the needs of people with dyslexia were better understood and met in the USA and Europe.

Over the period of time dyslexia has been researched, a number of theories have been proposed and a deal of conflict has resulted. In the 1990s a single phonological (auditory) deficit theory became dominant and attracted interest and funding. However, dyslexia is linked to a profile of difficulties and phonological descriptions alone are not enough as, in addition, skills unrelated to literacy may be affected.

Causes and current thinking

Dyslexia has multiple causes and manifestations and there is no single comprehensive definition of the condition that covers all the areas of difficulty that people face. Research into the syndrome has come from a variety of academic areas such as biology and psychology and there has been a great deal of investigation into the different areas (e.g. Carter 1998; Snowling and Stackhouse 2000). As a result, explanations of the syndrome operate on different levels explaining behaviour, the processing difficulties and differences in the structure and function of the brain. Each level underlies the other and all are needed for a full understanding of dyslexia.

Researchers have found that there are areas of symmetry in dyslexic brains where there is asymmetry in non-dyslexic ones. In addition, there are some areas that 'underperform' and others that are more active than in people without dyslexia. The main areas of the brain that are implicated are those controlling visual and auditory input, which process sight and sounds, the language processing areas and the area which controls motor (movement) input and output (Stephenson and Fairgrieve 1996).

Dyslexia is common in families. Differences in the make-up of the brain are believed to be affected by the immune system, which has been found to process essential fatty acids (like from fish) poorly (Stein 2001). As the immune system is affected there is a link to asthma, hay fever and allergies. Co-morbidity with other conditions such as ADHD and dyspraxia are common.

At present, knowledge of dyslexia is incomplete and research is ongoing. Currently, there is no real consensus on definition or cause. Progress has been made in theory, diagnosis, support and policy and each theory has its strengths and weaknesses. Integrated research using a multidisciplinary approach through international collaboration will result in unified theories with distinctions and commonalities

To understand current research and thinking, it is important to divide the information into three distinct areas: behavioural 'symptoms', the processing differences behind these and the underlying biology, which results in differences in processing (Frith 1997). It is clear that confusion about dyslexia, its causes and approaches to remediation has resulted from the complexity of information coming from these areas of study.

For example, initial descriptions of dyslexia centred purely upon difficulties in reading. These were later extended to writing and literacy in general. More recently, understanding of dyslexia has developed to the point that it is recognized as having a far wider ranging impact that affects all kinds of information processing. For instance, people with dyslexia often have difficulty telling left from right or remembering their way and older theories could not take into account effects like these.

Researchers from the field of cognitive psychology have developed theories to account for difficulties in the area of processing differences. These include a weakness in short-term working memory, which explain problems in holding and storing information. In this way difficulties in learning and remembering spellings can be understood.

A greater amount of debate has taken place at the biological level. Initially, it was thought that there were problems with the visual system itself (see Hinshelwood 1917). This was quickly found to be untrue and nowadays in order to be diagnosed with dyslexia the visual system must be working within normal limits. It has been shown that the difficulties lie in the processing of information, for example, in 'translating' the images seen when reading. Stein (2001) has found that people with dyslexia are affected by a mistiming of information input, which can cause blurring, or mixing of letters.

Over time, focus in research has moved between areas and, at times, there has been disagreement and even conflict. For example, the visual deficit theories described above were later overtaken by a theory that the primary difficulty was in processing auditory input (sound). For this reason it was believed that most problems with reading were to do with an inability to translate sounds to letters to words.

What is now understood is that the best explanations contain elements of all of the theories and should operate on all the levels. It is known that there are three main kinds of processing difficulty – visual, auditory and motor – and that these are caused by differences in the structure and function of the brain. Later we will see how this relates to theories on treatment and approaches to support and how no single approach will ever work for all people with dyslexia.

Diagnosis and assessment

The diagnostic process begins with referral, which can be made by a doctor, school, college, workplace or privately by the person thought to have dyslexia or their family. Initial screening will take place, which will look for 'indicators' of dyslexia. These include dyslexia or other related difficulties in the family, problems with remembering sequences like days, months and numbers and variety of other areas. If it is felt that the person may have dyslexia, they may go on to have a full assessment of some sort.

There are two distinct types of assessment: formal and support-based (for personal development). Formal assessments are usually administered by educational psychologists or qualified specialist teachers and are used for exam arrangements and other purposes needing an assessment recognized by the legal system. Support-based assessments tend to be undertaken in educational or workplace settings by appropriately qualified professionals and are intended primarily to provide information for the person affected and those working with them.

Both kinds of assessment provide information on strengths and weaknesses, but present the information in different ways. Formal assessments tend to include scaled measurements where the person's performance is compared to usual expectations for their age (see e.g. Wide Range Achievement Test, 3rd edition (WRAT-3)). Support assessments also provide comparison but do not tend to include age or scales, more descriptions of strengths and areas of difficulty.

The main difference in the two systems is that formal assessments may end simply with a statement of diagnosis detailing symptoms and root causes. In contrast, support assessments will go on to recommend support, equipment, or changes to tasks, activities and environment. Although they do not have full legal recognition, support assessments may be useful to the person with dyslexia and by others around them. Formal assessments may be funded privately, by schools, colleges or universities. Colleges, employers or individuals may pay for support assessments.

Formal and support assessments follow the same pattern, beginning with diagnostic interviews. These are designed to obtain an outline of the person's educational and medical history and details of type and severity of the difficulties faced. The interview is followed by a series of tests used to work out the underlying causes of the difficulties. They include reading and spelling assessments that show which kinds of strategies a person uses to attack these tasks as well as how well they can perform. Tests of ability in recognizing and splitting up sounds and working memory are also given.

After testing, the assessor will analyse the information from the interview and tests and write a report giving a detailed description of their findings. In the case of formal diagnosis this will primarily give percentile scores and measures contrasted against the general population. Support reports are more descriptive and discuss areas of skill and ability and areas in which the person has a weakness and needs support.

To avoid difficulties others have run into in assessing too narrowly, assessors measure dyslexia partly against criteria which do not fall into areas of contention. For example, tests cover a variety of processing areas and other cognitive operations like short-term memory. Also, dyslexia is defined by the discrepancy of skills in certain areas such as reading and spelling, against a general level of at least average ability. To be diagnosed with dyslexia a person must have an IQ of 90 or above; below this they will be assessed as having different kinds of difficulties or disabilities.

Characteristics

Dyslexia, like other neuro-diverse conditions, is a hidden disability and others may be unaware that the person they are dealing with has a difficulty which may affect many areas of their life. Children and adults with dyslexia can also be unaware that other people do not face the same problems they do in decoding text, following instructions, reading maps and such, so they may not even be clear about the extent of their difficulties themselves.

It may be most easy to spot in schools and other educational establishments that rely heavily on processing written and verbal information and so 'expose' the difficulties being faced. However, dyslexia can affect adults at least as much as children and others outside as well as within education and it can have a serious negative impact on their ability to maximize their potential or even live life without a daily struggle. Awareness and understanding can go a long way to developing strategies or making changes that can enhance people's experiences.

Typical characteristics can include the following:

- Visual memory problem affecting word recognition, i.e. someone who can read but persistently fails to recognize common words in print.

- Difficulty in learning from rules.

- Inconsistency, i.e. the person can spell something one day and makes an error the next.

- Noticeably 'good' and 'bad' days.

- Problems with reading (understanding or sounding out new words).

- Persistent severe spelling problems or erratic spellings.

- Difficulty in learning to tell the time on an analogue watch (one with hands).

- Poor pen control leading to hand strain, pressing hard on paper or poor hand-writing.

- Ambidexterity (not left or right handed).

- Left/right confusion.

- Problems memorizing things like the alphabet or multiplication tables.

- Quick forgetting, especially of names and specific words for things.

- Discrepancy between verbal and written performance.

- Difficulty in getting ideas on to paper and especially with starting things.

- Problems with sequential ordering (maths, sentences, paragraphs, essay structure) despite practice.

- Losing place in series or in reading.

- Confusion between letters and words.

- Letter reversals.

- Written work not expressing understanding, ideas or vocabulary fully.

- No, little or misplaced use of punctuation.

- Difficulty in seeing errors.

- Poor organization (of desk or work).

- Difficulty learning new information or following long instructions.

- Missed appointments and forgotten keys, equipment, etc.

- Jumbling speech.

Dyslexia can affect mathematical skills as poor short-term memory results in problems learning number bonds, multiplication tables, etc. Difficulties with the sequence of procedures and speed of information processing mean people with dyslexia do not have enough time to consolidate their learning before moving on. The language of maths questions can also prevent access.

In contrast people with dyslexia may have specific strengths and skills including the following:

- Creative/spatial flair (architecture, art, interior design, furniture making, engineering, construction, design in media, web design, theatre, fashion).

- Advanced global thinking resulting in good problem solving (politics, business strategies, advertising, media, information technology).

- Practical or physical dexterity (construction, sports coaching, carpentry).

- Good verbal communication (police, care work, public relations, teaching, training, giving presentations).

Implications

As dyslexia is often not diagnosed at all or diagnosed later in life (the majority of people are diagnosed after the age of 16: Brayton 1997) a common experience of education is failure, lack of understanding by others, humiliation and bullying. Misdiagnosis or lack of diagnosis can result in people developing emotional or behavioural symptoms from the frustration of being unable to demonstrate their skills fully. It may also affect self-esteem. Without effective strategies and support, people with dyslexia can fail to achieve at school, college and work, which can also impact on their mental health and emotional well-being.

A common outcome in employment is that people are unable to demonstrate their abilities in the form of qualifications or are afraid to potentially expose their weaknesses. Lack of opportunities may have prevented them from discovering their strengths and they may be aware only of areas of difficulty so they can end up in employment below the level of their skills and abilities. Alternatively, they may lose work or fail to fully achieve or get promoted, as they are unable to work to their potential.

By contrast, a person with dyslexia armed with a good understanding of their own particular skills and weaknesses and a set of strategies with which to approach them can be an incredible asset to an organization. Their ability to think holistically, make connections and visualize all sides of a problem can result in them developing novel responses to the issues in hand. For example, in the field of engineering, the superior three-dimensional modelling skills of dyslexic employees can enhance innovation and excellence in product design.

Dyslexia may affect a variety of areas in a person's life. For example, having trouble with reading and/or organization can affect paying bills, which can result in fines or even loss of property. Getting to and from appointments can be a challenge to someone who has difficulty telling the time, judging the passage of time, noting and remembering information and following directions. Authors have hypothesized that a possible reason for such a high percentage of people in prison having dyslexia (estimated at 50 per cent – Dyslexia Initiative Conference 2002) may be due to missed court dates, failure to read and follow instructions and procedures resulting in custodial sentences being awarded for even minor crimes.

Treatments and approaches

As might be expected with such a wide-ranging condition, there is a great variety in the types of treatments and approaches to remediation and support. Although great claims are sometimes made for a single method, the fact that there are a number of causes resulting in different characteristics or symptoms means that no one type will address all difficulties. As people may have visual, auditory or motor difficulties (or a combination of two or more) so the approach to treatment or support should be matched appropriately to their specific needs.

For example, in the past many people with dyslexia were not properly assessed and were assigned remedial classes and special schools. However, they failed to make expected progress, as the teaching methods used with learning difficulties are unsuited to dyslexia. On a more detailed level, the use of 'sounding out' strategies for a person with auditory processing difficulties is bound to result in lack of success in developing spelling and/or reading. Identification of the person's unique symptoms and assessment of their underlying causes is crucial to the development of effective and appropriate support.

Below is a brief overview of the types of treatment and support that have been developed and the types of difficulties they are best applied to.

Visual difficulties

Where these result in blurring, moving or swirling text, researchers observed effective improvement using eye patching, which prevents different information being input and processed through the two eyes (Stein 2001). Later on the patch can be removed and the stability remains. The Irlen system of overlays and lenses can be used to alleviate scotopic sensitivity. This is a difficulty in processing light frequencies, which can also affect reading as it causes the effects noted above and also glare, pulsing and other problems.

The methods described above reduce visual disturbance, thus helping with learning orthography (the order of letters) and assisting learning to read and spell.

Auditory difficulties

Where a person has auditory processing difficulties, they may have problems in distinguishing between sounds and identifying which sounds go with which letters. Phonological awareness methods are aimed at increasing sensitivity to transitions between sounds, improving awareness of the match between sounds and letters, therefore improving spelling and reading (Shaywitz 1996).

Motor difficulties

Following research which demonstrated deficiencies in the operation of the cerebellum (which controls gross and fine motor performance and sensory processing), remediators developed methods to improve this area of difficulty. A specific set of exercises was devised which aimed to improve the processing of input and output which would then assist in areas like reading, through better eye movement, writing, through hand–eye coordination and so on.

A number of other methods have also been promoted. For example, on a biological level, it is not possible to alter the structural make-up of the brain, but changes to its function may be achieved. As immune systems and poor ability to metabolize or retain polyunsaturated fatty acids (PUFAs) are implicated in a variety of difficulties, supplementation with essential fatty acids (EFAs) may help. The Davis system promotes dyslexia as a gift and operates by bringing dyslexic skills to bear on tasks often challenging to dyslexics (Davis 1994).

Earlier systems focused on a literacy model to develop what were seen as deficient skills in this area. Additional focus on these areas was thought to result in improved performance. However, as we have seen, a system which does not match appropriate methods to specifically identified difficulties will not achieve good results.

Self-help strategies

- Learn as much as you can about your strengths and weaknesses.

- Use strengths to support areas where you have more difficulty.

- Develop compensatory strategies like predicting the content of writing before reading, which will help you recognize more words in the text.

- Find a buddy or mentor at work who can support you in tasks you find difficult, like proofreading.

- Make sure you sleep well and reduce anxiety as much as possible as these impact negatively on short-term memory capacity.

- Try to eat oily fish, which is high in EPA (a polyunsaturated fatty acid), or take supplements because EFAs can help the brain function more effectively.

- Use active listening and reading methods (such as noting keywords in speech or thinking of questions before reading) to retain and understand information more effectively.

- Work with others to make notes, lists and schedules to support planning, organization and memory.

- Use mobiles, calendars, wall charts and personal organizers to provide focus and structure and remember deadlines.

Supporting strategies

- Break tasks into manageable and achievable chunks following logical paths to completion and success.

- Be understanding of forgetfulness and confusion, and be aware of difficulty in processing and remembering long or complex instructions.

- Present information in a variety of formats, such as drawing pictures and cartoons to allow people to use their range of skills and abilities, not just writing or verbal skills.

- Use overviews and mind-maps to enable people to see the whole as well as the parts and make use of visual and spatial thinking skills.

- Make sure you present the 'why' as well as the 'what' as people with dyslexia learn most effectively where information is meaningful.

- Appreciate that living with or knowing a person with dyslexia means that you may be dealing with a very creative individual who can be fun, exciting and spontaneous.

- Remember that people with dyslexia are often very good at seeing solutions and ways around a problem that other people would not think of and take advantage of this ability.

- Look at Chapters 11 and 12, where there are more strategies and ideas for supporting neuro-diverse people in education and work.

Words from those affected

Sam, diagnosed with dyslexia at the age of 28, shares her experiences:

I was diagnosed with dyslexia while studying on a part-time university course. The diagnosis brought clarity to so many situations and feelings that I've experienced in the past.

In year 4 of primary school [8–9 year group] I was put into a 'special needs' class because of my reading level. My parents were confused because I excelled in all other subjects and they fought with the school to have me moved into the mainstream class. During that year I received support for my reading, which brought it to the same level as my peers. However, the teacher needed to allocate me additional work in all other subjects because I completed the set work so quickly. Clearly this was at a time when dyslexia was not well recognized and there was an assumption that if you could not read and write to the expected standard, your overall ability was low. The following year I was moved into the mainstream class and I was more than able at keeping up with my peers.

In secondary school I did not receive any support and was in the highest groups for all subjects. My spelling was always a little ropey but my teachers discounted this because of my overall ability. In the final two years of secondary school I began to get bored and did not understand the relevance of what I was learning to my future. I always wanted to learn practical, applicable skills not theoretical ones and so I decided that school was not for me and stopped attending.

When returning my textbooks to school, my English teacher broke down in tears and explained how I could have achieved so much. Obviously at 15 I knew better! The school did let me sit four GCSEs [General Certificate of Secondary Education examinations], English, English Literature, maths and science. Despite not attending for over a year I achieved a grade C for my English Literature GCSE, which I am still very proud of.

After leaving school I had numerous jobs from waitressing to sales and finally business administration. I found that I got easily bored with daily duties; once I've mastered something I need to learn something else. I always wanted new responsibilities or the chance to use my own initiative. Quite often I would stop going to work and look for the next opportunity.

Between the ages of 17 and 19, I'd had over ten jobs and my family despaired of me. People thought that I was lazy and did not want to work but really I was bored and couldn't face doing a job which did not stimulate me in any way. I eventually completed two NVQs [National Vocational Qualifications], one in Business Administration and another in Customer Service. These were the first qualifications that I enjoyed undertaking because they were practical.

I had my first child at 21 and it was then that I decided I needed to gain some more qualifications. How could I teach my children the importance of education when I had flunked out myself? I enrolled on an Access to Higher Education course and successfully completed it, though I found it amazingly difficult. I decided that full-time study at university was not for me and began working in the college that I had attended, supporting people with learning difficulties and disabilities. It was the perfect role for me because the young people who I was working with were like me at that age. I could understand their frustration and help them to achieve.

Through training and experience I developed in my role and started teaching. I didn't get bored because every day was different and I was always learning something new. However, I needed to complete a teaching course at university to be able to do my job. I struggled in my first year and finished it with difficulty. Again I could not organize myself and found it difficult to get the information in my head onto the paper.

In the second year of the course my friend suggested that I might be dyslexic and I had an assessment with an educational psychologist, which confirmed my dyslexia. I felt quite proud when it was confirmed: I work with dyslexic people and I have always admired their commitment and determination, now I was 'in the club'. I freely tell my students that I have dyslexia and how proud I am to have it. I feel that it encourages and inspires learners; look at Richard Branson!

The diagnosis explained so many things to me, like why my brain could do things but they didn't come out right when I tried to explain them. Sometimes it felt like so much was going on up there and I knew I could do so much but I couldn't demonstrate my abilities, as I was unable to express myself.

It felt like my brain was a prisoner in my skull, desperate to show people what it could do but this net was restricting its potential. Sometimes I still feel like this but I have started to learn how to convey myself better and it has really helped with the frustrations that I have experienced in the past.

I believe my dyslexia is a gift and there are many strengths attached to it. My educational psychologist assessment showed that I have exceptional skills in perceptual organization; they were recorded at the 98th percentile, which is in the top 0.04 per cent of the population. This explained why I am good at parking the car: I've always been good at visualizing whether my car would fit into a space and getting it in there. I like to try and park in the smallest possible spaces to challenge myself; my friends think I'm mad but I really enjoy 'achieving the impossible'.

This also fits in with my ability to make flat pack furniture without the instructions. I know that it is a very dyslexic trait to jump in head first, but I really don't need the instructions, I visualize in my mind how it will all fit together. I realized that I was good at fitting shapes together when I was at school and we would build the nest of three dimensional shapes. In hindsight I wish that I had known about this at school because I could have developed my skills into a career. It is something that I would still like to do because I enjoy working with shapes, space, two and three dimensions.

My dyslexia also means that I have an ability to think differently from others and bring alternative views to the table. For example when I've been involved with changes I am able to look at situations from a different perspective. I can see how things could be improved or developed but find it difficult to write step-by-step plans on how this can be achieved. However, I get frustrated with people who cannot keep up with my thinking. When I visualize a solution I cannot understand why other people need to build on their thoughts to understand what I can visualize immediately.

I have my weaknesses like everyone else, but since my diagnosis I have been more aware of my dyslexic traits. I leave everything until the last minute, like writing essays, planning for lessons, doing the food shopping. I have the best intentions in the world but I cannot organize myself; my brain is thinking about the next thing before I can get the present thing done. I really have to discipline myself to carry anything out until the end, without stopping. It's the way that I am and I am aware of it so I make sure I plan for my low boredom levels.

I speak really quickly because it's hard for my mouth to keep up with my brain. My friends have got used to me now, but when I meet new people I see them get lost during conversations with me. Something that has really helped to 'slow me down' is my teaching, because the learners that I teach need time to process new information and I make sure that I am aware of the speed I am speaking or teaching at. I have also given presentations in public, which need to be delivered at a slow steady pace. I have had to spend hours practising this pacing.

One of my really big weaknesses is taking on too much and I can't judge the impact on time or energy levels. I need to use a diary and notebook religiously to keep track of things, my memory is not very good and I need to write everything down. I've learned that when I have a lot to do or remember, I need to keep lists and stick to them. I can get overwhelmed and having a list makes me feel like I have control of things.

There are always going to be words that I'm going to have difficulty spelling, like the word 'vehicle', which will never stick in my mind, and pages in books that I'll need to reread because when I get to the bottom I realize that I've understood, but not retained the meaning. I know my weaknesses and I have strategies to help me improve. Still, sometimes I don't use the strategies because I'm tired or lazy or haven't got the time.

I'm very lucky because a lot of my friends have good knowledge and understanding of dyslexia and they constantly offer me support and encouragement. As my son has got older, I have learned that he also has difficulties with literacy although he has strong abilities in many other areas. Now I know how to support and nurture him because of my own experiences.

CHAPTER 5

Dyspraxia (Developmental Coordination Disorder)

I used to get labelled as being careless and lazy at school and that I wasn't trying hard enough. I have a hidden disability so some people make assumptions about my lack of intelligence.

Introduction

Once known as 'clumsy child syndrome', dyspraxia is a condition which affects coordination, movement, balance and also information processing. A person with dyspraxia will typically find many aspects of daily life difficult as it relies so much on being able to manipulate the physical environment. Dyspraxia, known as developmental coordination disorder in the USA, can affect handwriting, walking, getting dressed, using keys, tying laces, driving and a multitude of other things. Alongside the physical coordination aspects, those with dyspraxia often exhibit characteristics akin to other neuro-diverse conditions, particularly Asperger syndrome and ADHD (Colley 2006). These are particularly in areas such as short-term memory, concentration, social interaction and sequencing.

Many adults remain undiagnosed and yet may experience significant difficulties and frustrations, not knowing why life seems such a trial for them. Some people report that others perceive them as 'stupid' as they seem to be unable to quickly carry out tasks and instructions that other people find simple. This is generally the result of an information processing difficulty rather than low intelligence or capability. As with other neuro-diverse conditions, there are increasing numbers of adults who are embracing their dyspraxia and feel that it is very much part of who they are.

History

Dyspraxia has been documented under the terms congenital maladroitness, clumsy child syndrome, developmental coordination disorder (DCD), clumsiness, developmental dyspraxia, developmental disorder of motor function. The notion of developmental clumsiness has been discussed since the 1930s (Orton 1937), but it is only in recent years that we have a full understanding of how this condition affects individuals. Sasson Gubbay's work in the 1970s first identified a condition which involved motor and movement impairments in children with no accompanying learning disability (Gubbay 1975), which we now understand as dyspraxia. The term 'dyspraxia' derives from the Greek 'praxis', which means 'doing' or 'acting' accompanied by 'dys', which means impaired.

Causes and current thinking

Dyspraxia is said to be caused by an immature development of parts of the brain which lead to a reduced number of connections between nerve cells (Portwood 1999). This would explain the additional time required for those with dyspraxia to process instructions and also their less precise limb control. It may be that dyspraxia is caused by similar neurological causes to other neuro-diverse conditions, as characteristics are similar and co-morbidity (overlap) with other conditions is very common. There is thought to be a strong familial link in dyspraxia with other family members more likely to experience characteristics than in non-dyspraxic families.

Diagnosis and assessment

Diagnosis or assessment should be carried out by a qualified and experienced practitioner, often an occupational, educational or clinical psychologist. This can be through referral from a medical practitioner, through work or college, or privately funded. There are limited numbers of people fully experienced in diagnosing adult dyspraxia, so ensuring that the clinician selected has the skills to do the job is very important. Many individuals choose to self-diagnose and feel this is sufficient for them to have self-knowledge and awareness.

The diagnostic process will vary according to the clinician, but should include a full developmental history from childhood. Ages at which the person walked, talked and gained motor coordination skills are important indicators for possible dyspraxia. For the majority of people, the indicators and signs of dyspraxia will have been evident since early childhood. There may also be hand-writing and motor skills tests and activities to measure performance, along with psychometric tests to measure intelligence and other cognitive abilities.

Adults with dyspraxia report anecdotally that they are not always taken seriously by professionals when seeking diagnosis. They may be told that everyone has these elements and be quite dismissive. It is important to be clear about the range and extent of the difficulties that you have – perhaps writing them down to take to the appointment to give a full picture of the impact.

The DSM-IV (APA 1994) refers to dyspraxia as developmental coordination disorder and a summary of the main criteria is as follows:

- There is marked impairment in the development of motor coordination.

- The difficulties are significant in everyday and/or academic functioning.

- The characteristics seen are not due to a medical or physical condition.

- Characteristics are not due to a pervasive developmental disorder such as autism or Asperger syndrome.

These criteria do not mention the perceptual and processing difficulties that many people face and so perhaps are not a full representation of the true experience of the condition, which, of course, is very likely to be overlapping with at least one, if not more, other neuro-diverse conditions.

Characteristics

People with dyspraxia experience the characteristics in a wide spectrum of severity and variety, which may vary from day to day or situation to situation, and which tend to be more pronounced when stress levels are high.

Childhood indicators

A developmental history will include questions relating to the person's behaviour as a child. A sample of typical features of dyspraxia in childhood are:

- difficulty in dressing oneself – putting on socks, doing up buttons

- crawling or standing later than other children

- sensitivity to the environment – particularly to sound or light

- often tripping over, bumping into things, general lack of balance

- poor hand grip and hand–eye coordination

- difficulty in learning to ride a bike

- difficulty in catching a ball.

Adult indicators

The childhood characteristics listed above may still apply in adulthood; some adults with dyspraxia will be unable to catch a ball or ride a bike and many report that clumsiness and minor accidents are a daily occurrence. Despite the focus here on the negative impact of dyspraxia, many individuals with this condition are highly creative, unique personalities, who have carved careers and successful lives for themselves and see their condition as being a vital part of this success. The following characteristics are summarized from Mary Colley's excellent book, *Living with Dyspraxia* (2006), which provides in-depth advice for adults with the condition.

Gross motor skills – big movements involving the whole body

- Lack of rhythm which affects ability to engage in dance, sports and exercise.

- Clumsy walking style, running style and general body movement – a lack of 'grace'.

- Difficulty in making changes to direction and movement.

- Bumping into things, falling over.

- Poor coordination of left/right sides of body, making activities such as cycling difficult.

- Poor hand–eye coordination, which may make driving difficult.

Fine motor skills – small movements involving individual parts of the body

- Difficulty with any task that involves delicate manipulation of objects, such as sewing, using cutlery, putting keys in locks.

- Difficulty with dressing and personal care, including fastening clothes, applying make-up or shaving. May appear scruffy and unkempt. Clothes may be creased and unironed.

- Person may have poor hand-writing and find hand-writing painful and frustrating.

Language and perception

- Speech difficulties – person may find clear speech difficult and may muddle words and meanings. Difficulties with pitch, speed and volume of speech may also be present.

- Unusual and engaging speaker – those with dyslexia can be a 'different' personality, which is interesting and attractive to listen to.

- Visual difficulties – sensitivity to light, squinting, rapid blinking and difficulties in tracking text or objects are likely in a person with dyspraxia.

- Sensitivity to noise, which may make certain environments painful or impossible to function in. This will be sensitivity beyond that considered within the average range.

- Sensitivity to touch, which may manifest as a dislike of clothing or being touched or held by other people.

- Poor perception of time, direction, speed or distance.

Executive functioning – planning and organization

- Poor short-term memory – the person forgets where things are and where they are supposed to be.

- Difficulty in maintaining concentration – may switch from one activity to another, but not complete these adequately.

- Procrastination – may struggle to begin a task and wander aimlessly.

- May find organization difficult and live in a chaotic, cluttered environment.

- Original thinker – creative problem-solver.

Implications

People with dyspraxia can suffer from anxiety and low self-esteem due to being constantly aware that they might create a problem, through misunderstanding communication, knocking something over or not being able to participate in physical activities. Friendships and relationships can be difficult as those with dyspraxia can find social chat difficult and can struggle to remain focused on one topic, or may speak very quickly. They may be seen as rude for interrupting and appear not to listen to others. Difficulties with the reading of non-verbal signals such as body language and eye contact mean that subtle communication messages may be missed and an incorrect assessment of the situation made. If someone has experienced repeated failures or rejections, they may start to avoid certain situations to ensure no further mishaps. This can result in isolation and an increasing lack of confidence.

Gaining academic qualifications may be difficult for those who have attention and processing issues, which may lead to unsatisfying work, which is beneath the capabilities of the person. If you cannot prove that you are able, it can be hard to convince an employer that you are up to the job. It may also be problematic for the person to present themselves appropriately for interviews or work if they have motor difficulties with dressing and grooming.

As with many neuro-diverse conditions, many individuals are intelligent and able but their achievements, manner and appearance may lead others to think otherwise and believe that this is a result of laziness and lack of care, rather than due to a developmental difference.

Treatments and approaches

There is no treatment for dyspraxia in its entirety, but there are interventions that can support aspects of dyspraxia.

Counselling and other forms of therapy

A late diagnosis of dyspraxia can be an emotional experience. Some people feel a great relief that the reason for their past difficulties has been identified, but others may feel angry at the missed opportunities, failures and rejections that they have experienced. This can occur over an extended period after the diagnosis, but should in time lead to acceptance of the new knowledge.

Living with dyspraxia can cause low confidence and self-esteem, often due to the reactions of others who don't understand. Counselling can help to put these feelings into perspective. Cognitive behavioural therapy can also be helpful as a practical way of learning new ways to perceive oneself and limit harmful thoughts and beliefs. The Further Reading section has information on books on this subject.

Educational support

Additional support is available for those with disabilities studying at school or college. This may be additional time for exams, alternative assessment methods or a support worker to take notes or assist with practical tasks where dyspraxia impairs the person's ability to do so. Individual learning support may be available to teach strategies for improving information processing, planning essays and organizing time.

Visual difficulties

For those who experience visual difficulties, specialist optometrists can provide tests and coloured lenses which can ease some of the discomfort. A condition called scotopic sensitivity is related to dyspraxia and dyslexia.

Sensory sensitivity

For information on sensory sensitivity, which is sometimes experienced by those with dyspraxia, see Chapter 3 on autistic spectrum conditions.

Physiotherapy and occupational therapy

Physiotherapy and occupational therapy may help with improving physical coordination and devising tools and methods for overcoming specific difficult areas. This will probably need to be sought privately and may be costly.

Self-help strategies

- Remember that self-acceptance is crucial for someone with dyspraxia. This will help you to not get so angry and frustrated with yourself when you bump into something or struggle to perform a task which others would find simple.

- Join a support group – meeting others who face similar daily challenges can feel very reassuring. They may have found solutions to problems that would be helpful to you.

- Ensure that you have an eye test carried out to identify any visual perception difficulties and get appropriate glasses. Coloured transparent overlays which change the background colour of the page can be very helpful.

- Use colour-coded filing systems and memory aids to help with organization and appointments.

- Do things slowly without rushing to avoid accidents and clumsiness.

- Focus on developing your areas of ability, such as creative thinking, problem solving and your unique view of the world.

- Assess the home, school or work environment for practical tools and aids that make physical functioning easier. Mary Colley's (2006) book, as mentioned above, has entire sections dedicated to detailing issues in the office, the kitchen, travelling and many others and practical ways to overcome them. These are some examples of practical solutions for daily problems:

- Buy a dishwasher if you break a lot of plates when washing up.

- Keep your home as clutter free as possible to help with keeping things tidy and not tripping over things.

- Choose a vacuum cleaner that you can operate and manoeuvre easily.

- Label bottles and jars clearly, so you know what is in them.

- Keep sharp knives stored safely and away from other cutlery.

Supporting strategies

- Offer support with planning and organization. Make sure the person has calendars, schedules, alarms and diaries to aid short-term memory.

- Provide patience and acceptance – the person with dyspraxia is experiencing a lot more frustration with their behaviour than you are.

- Remember that some people with visual difficulties may require computer monitors to be adjusted to a different background colour.

- Allow use of computer, as hand-writing may be tiring and unclear.

- Support the person in maintaining a clear working area.

- With regards to support with studying and learning, refer to supporting strategies section in Chapter 4 on dyslexia, as many of the information processing difficulties are common to both. Chapter 11 on the learning environment has additional ideas for supporting learners with neuro-diversity.

Words from those affected

Janet, an adult with dyspraxia, shares her experiences:

I feel that having dyspraxia has made life more challenging and difficult than if I was neuro-typical. However, besides not being very good at copying other people's movements in dance and sports and being disorganized with my household chores, I find that it is society's lack of understanding of living with dyspraxia and their judgemental attitude that has caused me to have negative feelings about my dyspraxia.

My dyspraxia affects me socially in that I sometimes blurt things out without thinking first as I would forget what I'm going to say and interrupt people in conversation, which can be misinterpreted as being rude. I have offended people with my lack of tact, my sometimes loud speaking voice and my forthrightness, but in fact I was very shy and awkward in social situations. This has improved as I have gained more self-confidence. I also have difficulties eating with my mouth closed, which can cause offence.

In terms of motor skills and abilities, I find dancing and competitive sports socially exclude me if other people take dancing and sport seriously or are competitive about their team winning. I don't like joining in games like pool even with understanding people, because I can't even hold a cue properly or hit the ball.

I was a very sensitive child. I knew that I found physical education and spelling difficult and I was different and considered inferior to the other children. I cried a lot out of frustration because I found lessons difficult and when I was bullied, I had not learned to toughen up or fight back. I remember once being afraid to go home as I had received a really poor report and 'ran away' to my friend's house. My reports usually said 'could do better'.

In the first year of secondary school I was still considered to be a cry baby. I got frustrated because I found it hard to find my way around school and remember which rooms lessons were in. In primary school most lessons had been in the same room. I was put in the remedial class in the first year of a secondary modern [non-academic] school for girls. I found it very frustrating that marks were given for copying the teachers' work neatly off the blackboard and not for original thought. It was difficult for me to write neatly, copy accurately and spell. I was constantly bullied by my peers and was not popular with the boys, because I was overweight from comfort eating, wore spectacles and often looked miserable.

I found that I was not as thick as I thought I was and found the work too easy. Although I did begin to toughen up and became the class clown, which got me more accepted by my peers. I left school with six CSEs [certificate of secondary education] and my career adviser recommended that because I was 'non-academic', I should go into catering, which proved to be totally unsuitable. I did some bakery courses, finding the theory easier than the practical, and had problems with speed, manual dexterity and multitasking. When I worked in the hotel industry, I was told several times that I was a lovely person but I was just not suitable.

I used to have low self-esteem, anxiety and depression and consider myself to be a failure as a person in every way. I lived on incapacity benefit for eight years because I believed myself to be unemployable and stuck in a benefits trap. Some of my university tutors on the Diploma in Community and Youth Work and the PGCE [postgraduate certificate in education] got really frustrated with me because they believed in my abilities more than I did.

I have become a much more contented and confident person

as I have got older. I set up Dyspraxia Adult Action in Manchester to prove to myself that I wasn't completely useless. It has been very successful and has now evolved into Manchester Adult Neurodiversity Action. I studied on the Diploma in Community and Youth Work Studies at Manchester University and have been told by my tutors that my work was of a consistently high standard. I continued my studies on the degree in Community Studies at the University of Bolton. I then went on their Designing Futures Project for Disabled Graduates in Bolton and I was given advice on setting up my own Dyspraxia Inclusive training business. I then very smoothly completed the PGCE in the post-16 sector.

While working part time as a travel trainer I now raise awareness of dyspraxia professionally and I am finishing an MA in Inclusion and SEN [special educational needs] at Manchester Metropolitan University. I received help with structuring my Assignments and Specialist software and a computer with my Disabled Student's Allowance and asked for an extension on my assignments only when it was necessary.

I used to get labelled as being careless and lazy at school and that I wasn't trying hard enough. I have a hidden disability so some people make assumptions about my lack of intelligence. On the other hand, others often consider me to be highly intelligent so they don't understand why I have difficulties with short-term memory and manual dexterity and why I lose my possessions so frequently. People often don't understand why I mention that I have dyspraxia as it makes them feel uncomfortable and tell me that there's 'nothing wrong with me' and that I am 'more normal than a normal person' (whatever that is supposed to mean). The one thing that really annoys me is people who are patronizing and talk to me like I am stupid when I know that I am more capable than they are.

As I have a good sense of humour and quick verbal wit, many people find me a good laugh. I have found that I can relate to people that other people cannot relate to, such as people with disabilities and people with enduring mental health issues and other so-called hard-to-reach people who have been socially excluded. I have empathy with groups of oppressed people, outstanding creative, multi-sensory teaching ability and can solve problems outside the box. These are the positive aspects of my dyspraxia and who I am.

Janet's hints on self-esteem

- Learn to love yourself, no one is perfect.

- Concentrate on your strengths rather than your difficulties.

- Don't compare yourself with other people.

- Recognize your own achievements, especially if you were ever bullied, criticized or ostracized by other people.

- Don't beat yourself up by thinking whatever you do it's not as good as what other people do.

- Keep a sense of humour no matter how embarrassed you get, even if you come out of the toilet of a posh hotel, with your flies open or your skirt tucked into your knickers, and you are the last to notice.

- Change putdowns into positive comments.

- Receive compliments gracefully. Smile, say thank you, then shut up.

CHAPTER 6

Dyscalculia (Mathematic Disorder)

I do sometimes have an intuitive sense as to whether I have been over- or under-charged for something without being able to calculate it. I often have a sense of what region an answer will be in even if I don't understand the calculation.

Introduction

Dyscalculia tends to appear combined with another neuro-diverse condition, such as ADHD, dyspraxia or a learning disability. I have yet to meet anyone who just experiences only this condition and has no other difficulties with learning and information processing. Often it is not even mentioned as an individual condition, but is deemed to be an inherent aspect of another condition, usually dyslexia, dyspraxia or ADHD.

Dyscalculia, also know as mathematics disorder in the DSM-IV (APA 1994), is a difficulty with the concepts of number. This is not simply someone who may be 'bad at maths', it is more than that. The other distinguishing feature, similar to dysgraphia, is that the mathematical ability should be significantly different from that expected by the person's age, education level or intelligence. A person with dyscalculia may be highly skilled verbally and yet not be able to determine whether 4 or 9 is the larger number.

History

The first major study identifying a distinct, neurological mathematical disorder was written by Kosc (1974) and some work has been carried out since, but dyscalculia remains largely unresearched and exact causes remain unclear. Dyscalculia was first recognized in the UK in 2001 (Department for Education and Skills (DfES) 2001). Prevalence is estimated at between 1 and 7 per cent of the population (Parliamentary Office of Science and Technology 2004) and there is evidence to suggest that there is a genetic link due to the high occurrence of dyscalculia in the members of the same family.

Causes and current thinking

There is debate as to how much dyscalculia is specifically related to dyslexia or dyspraxia, even though it is often grouped with these conditions and not identified as an individual issue. Difficulties with sequencing and coordination are seen in those with ADHD, dyslexia and dyspraxia and, as with most neuro-diverse conditions, it is not usually seen in isolation, but in conjunction with other conditions. It is usually first seen in children around the time of learning maths at school, but in adults incidence of dyscalculia can occur after brain injury. Undoubtedly, it is a neurological condition and for those who are affected throughout their lifetime (as opposed to acquired dyscalculia through brain injury), other family members are likely to be similarly affected. There is little research that has been carried out on dyscalculia and so not a great deal is yet known about this individual condition or exactly how many people are affected.

It is important to differentiate between dyscalculia and those with general low mathematical ability. There may be many reasons why an adult may not be good at maths – confidence, poor teaching, stigma about enjoying maths from peers. Basic concepts of number such as size and ordering may be easily understood by someone with low numeracy skills and not understood by someone with dyscalculia, whose general ability level may be higher.

Diagnosis and assessment

Dyscalculia can be diagnosed only by a qualified person. This is a less well known condition and finding a knowledgeable clinician may be difficult. An educational psychologist is likely to be the most relevant person to carry out the assessment. The diagnostic process involves a number of mathematical tests, which can determine the expected ability of the person and compare this to the actual ability observed. These conditions do not have a clear set of criteria by which they can be assessed and will rely on the expertise of the assessor to determine the presence and severity of the characteristics experienced.

A developmental history should also be taken to determine any additional difficulties or conditions and also assess the time of onset of the condition. It is important to rule out any other possible causes for the difficulty, for example, a learning disability may make literacy and numeracy more difficult and similarly, problems with vision could affect the ability to calculate and identify numbers effectively.

The diagnostic criteria of dyscalculia, as stipulated by the DSM-IV (APA 1994), states that mathematical skills are below what would be expected for the person's age, intelligence and education level. To receive a positive diagnosis, the difficulties have to be significant enough to cause an impact on academic or other areas of life.

In order to be eligible for additional support, educational or otherwise, an assessment may be required as proof of the level of need.

Characteristics

It is suggested that there may be many types of dyscalculia, affecting different aspects of mathematical understanding. Typical characteristics observed may be difficulties in the following areas:

- aligning numbers in sums
- reading and/or writing numbers
- understanding what is required in word-based mathematical problems
- remembering correct appointment times
- recalling car registration numbers
- making errors when writing cheques
- buying clothes in the correct size
- converting from one number system to another
- grasping the concept of size order in numbers
- memorizing multiplication tables
- understanding graphically presented data
- understanding the implications of results
- remembering and/or dialling phone numbers in the correct order
- memorizing names of geometrical shapes
- working out time on a 24-hour clock
- converting foreign currency when on holiday
- understanding commonly taught rules, such as fractions, decimal places, common mathematical symbols +, -, x, /
- keeping track of time and planning time-bound tasks
- sequencing and order.

Implications

Low confidence and self-esteem are common for those with dyscalculia due to a difficulty in being able to carry out simple mathematical calculations. Low academic achievement and high dropout rates are probable outcomes due to the emphasis on mathematical ability in learning.

Low mathematical ability is said to be more of problem in the workplace than low literacy ability (Bynner and Parsons 1997). As can be seen in the personal account at the end of this chapter, maths is present in many environments and for those lacking basic skills in this area, this can lead to leaving jobs, low self-esteem and problems with punctuality, financial planning and transactions involving money. For some people, buying a ticket for a train, planning the journey using timetables and then making sure that they are on time to catch the train would be impossible or very stressful. This has major implications for independent living and the ability to study or work any distance from home.

Treatments and approaches

There is no one accepted method for supporting dyscalculia, although early intervention for children is advised. For those in adulthood, modification approaches may be too late to make a significant difference and management strategies may be more practical. For those seeking intervention, education specialists working within the area of learning difficulties, such as dyslexia and dyspraxia, will be able to provide specific strategies for support, which may help to address the root cause, rather than manage difficult situations. It is important for the person with dyscalculia to come to terms with the fact that they have many skills and abilities, but are disabled by society's expectations of ability and that if they can find strategies to minimize their difficulties, then it is hoped that they will feel less frustrated.

Self-help strategies

- Use a calculator – carry a small one with you wherever you go, to work out change and costs.

- Enrol in an adult numeracy class at your local college. It is never too late to increase your understanding. You will be surprised at how many adults struggle with maths.

- Use timers and alarms to help with meeting appointments and timekeeping.

- Use children's books and websites as multi-sensory resources for learning basic concepts.

- Learn maths as an adult, which may be easier without the pressure of classmates and an impatient teacher. Some of your difficulties may be related to a lack of confidence from your school days – things might be different now.

Supporting strategies

- Do not assume that even basic mathematical concepts such as addition or number order are understood.

- Use visual, tactile or other sensory means to embed concepts.

- Identify the person's areas of strength and encourage these.

- If the person doesn't understand what you are explaining, find a new way to teach this topic.

- Do not assume a lack of intelligence or other ability. Dyscalculia does not indicate this at all.

- Identify preferred learning methods by questioning and observation.

- Avoid comments on neatness or minor errors as these may erode confidence further.

- Build confidence by praising success. This is likely to be a person with negative experiences of number usage.

- Teach rules and provide concrete examples and tools. Abstract concepts may be harder to grasp.

- Test for understanding. Don't just ask – the person will say 'yes' even if they haven't understood to avoid embarrassment.

Words from those affected

Lily, who has dyscalculia, talks about how it has affected her:

I was diagnosed ten years ago, when I was in my forties. I was at university at the time and my tutor noticed I was having difficulty learning grammar patterns in English, which uses the same part of the brain as mathematics. I was referred for an assessment and dyscalculia was diagnosed.

I have a very high verbal and reading ability and an IQ of 150+, putting me into the gifted range. I have a real affinity for words and was the first in my class at school to learn to read. I was thrown out of maths class at the age of 13 as I couldn't do long multiplication or division. This meant that I wasn't able to continue studying biology and botany, subjects that I was really excited by, because I couldn't do the maths involved. It was very frustrating to have a high ability in one area and not be able to do anything involving numbers. My teachers assumed I was just lazy: 'If you can learn spelling tables, why can't you learn your times tables?' I remember having to stand up in class and recite my times tables, which were taught by rote learning and repetition. I was slow at this and used my fingers. Having the teacher roll her eyes at me and hearing the sniggers of my classmates lowered my self-esteem.

My dyscalculia also affects me socially due to my inability to recognize faces, as this is a form of symbol recognition – the same as number. When I see someone in a different context from when I last saw them, it takes me a moment to work out who they are. This is long enough for them to realize that I haven't recognized them and they think that perhaps I don't want to talk to them or feel offended that I have forgotten who they are. I was also unable to play cards as a child as I can't keep track. Any game which involves planning a strategy, like chess or draughts, is impossible. I can only play board games which rely on luck. As a teenager, I found going to dances painful as I am unable to hear the beat or keep to a rhythm, which is part of dyscalculia. Other people tried to show me, but gave up when I couldn't learn the steps. This made it difficult for me to socialize.

Time is a big problem. I didn't learn to tell the time until I was 11 years old when I was given a wristwatch as a gift and decided to teach myself. Immediately after I had taught myself to tell the time, I was sorry I had done so. My concept of a day had changed. Before, if I had wanted to start something, I would have just started it, but once I knew what time was, I became unsure if I could complete the activity in the time I had and so became reluctant to start anything. This caused me some anxiety.

I still struggle to know how much time is in an hour and what I would be able to achieve in that time. When I am going to an appointment, I have no concept that I may be late until the time I am supposed to be there. I cannot work out that I won't be able to get there on time before this moment. This can make me seem selfish and as though I don't care about being late. My self-esteem is already low and then I feel guilty and annoyed with myself. If it is something like a doctor's appointment, I know I cannot be seen, as that is inconvenient to others and so I have to make another appointment and do the whole thing again another day. It all becomes a big mess.

When I go shopping, I can't calculate change. I don't know how much to expect back. When I am trying to work out calculations, it feels as though my brain is a lump of lead. It just won't work; it just sits there. I tend to go shopping at quiet times, when no one else is there. I take a list which I do not deviate from as I don't know if I will have enough money for anything else. I prefer to go to smaller shops, rather than large supermarkets, as I get disorientated and lost easily and cannot find what I am looking for. If I turn right to walk into a shop, when I come out, instead of turning left to go back where I came from, I will turn right again. I get an awful feeling that I don't know where I am. I laugh about it when I am with others, but it does make me wary of going shopping by myself and so I tend to go shopping with someone else. This makes me look needy and I don't want to look needy.

I carry a tiny calculator with me wherever I go, as well as my shopping list. I am afraid to spend money and have a lot of anxiety about financial planning, as I don't know how much money I will need. I have recently bought a house and taken on a mortgage, which I find terrifying. This big sum of money goes out every month and I have no idea if I have enough left to buy anything I need.

I have a tendency to lose things and so I attach everything I carry to me. I write everything down as I know I won't remember it and have a personal organizer and calendar with me to write down arrangements. I have trouble with days of the week, months, how many days there are in a month and what number month it is. I have a watch which shows me the time, day and date to help me with this. I don't know if I am on a Wednesday or a Friday otherwise.

I have only told members of my family and friends that I felt would understand about my diagnosis. Not all of them would be, so I needed to be selective. Some would use it as a weapon to mock me, rather than a route to understanding. I am afraid of people thinking I am stupid or lazy and then this fear clouds my perception.

I was unable to follow my interest in botany and biology for a career and was also unable to be a gardener as I didn't have the maths required to go to horticultural college. I have had to rely on my English abilities to get work. Whichever job I have had, there is always a requirement for maths, whether it be collecting money or completing a timesheet. I have done all sorts of jobs – taxi driver, retail, Christmas tree factory and a librarian. When things become too tedious or involve maths, where I would be seen to be 'stupid', I decide that I would rather leave than get fired and so I quit. I haven't told my employers that I have this disability as I have been able to talk my way into the job. It is only once I am doing the job that the problems crop up. I have studied to master's degree level and would like to use my high IQ and ability, but it is getting harder for me to find work as my CV is such a strange mixture of jobs.

I think that people don't understand dyscalculia and I am happy for people to ask me about it if they genuinely want to get information about it. Having dyscalculia doesn't mean that I am stupid and I don't want to be patronized.

I would like to be better at maths and be rid of some of the negative aspects of my dyscalculia, although I would like to keep my language and reading abilities. I'd like to see the world get rid of time. I can tell the time more or less by the sun and if people weren't so precise about time, it wouldn't matter so much if I was late.

CHAPTER 7

Dysgraphia (Disorder of Written Expression)

Everyone is wired in different ways. If you want to group people with similarities, fair enough, but don't persecute them for it. If my brain didn't work this way I'd still have gifts and problems – they'd just be different.

Introduction

Dysgraphia, also known as disorder of written expression in the DSM-IV (APA 1994), is a difficulty in writing which does not reflect the general intelligence and ability of the person. It is rarely seen in isolation and is usually accompanied by other conditions. It is generally thought to be a motor coordination difficulty, but there can be associated difficulties with processing and sequencing, such as letter formation, confusion of letters, particularly 'b' and 'd' for example, and also with other fine motor skills issues, such as tying shoelaces.

The difficulties experienced by people with dyspraxia often stem from the strong emphasis in the written word in educational assessments, which can cause low achievement despite an academic capability. Low self-esteem and confidence can also be the result of an awareness that writing ability is lower than expected.

History

There is nothing written specifically about the history of dysgraphia, as it is a little known condition. It is usually associated with dyspraxic motor skills difficulties or dyslexic reading issues. Orton (1937) wrote:

> In the normal adult, the various functions that make up the language faculty – speaking, reading, writing – are so closely interlinked, both in learning and by usage, that any interference with one seems prone to cause disturbance of the others. (p.24)

Causes and current thinking

Dysgraphia is also known as disorder of written expression, motor agraphia, developmental agraphia or special writing ability. The exact causes of dysgraphia are unknown, but are likely to be similar to other neuro-diverse conditions, therefore including genetic factors, brain injury or other illness. When seen in children, there are likely to be others with dysgraphia within the family. For those who acquire the condition in adulthood, brain injury or damage is the most probable cause. Due to the overlapping functions of the brain which affect more than just hand-writing, it may be impossible to isolate dysgraphia from other learning difficulties (Orton 1937).

Diagnosis and assessment

The information here is basically the same as it is for dyscalculia, although less is written and known about dysgraphia, as many people do not consider it a separate condition, but simply a characteristic of another condition, such as dyslexia or dyspraxia. This is important when considering diagnosis and the opinion of the clinician. Dysgraphia can be diagnosed only by a qualified person. This is a less well known condition and finding a knowledgeable clinician may be difficult. An educational psychologist is likely to be the most relevant person to carry out the assessment. The diagnostic process involves a number of mathematical tests, which can determine the expected ability of the person and compare this to the actual ability observed. These conditions do not have a clear set of criteria by which they can be assessed and will rely on the expertise of the assessor to determine the presence and severity of the characteristics experienced.

A developmental history should also be taken to determine any additional difficulties or conditions and also assess the time of onset of the condition. It is important to rule out any other possible causes for the difficulty, for example, any condition or illness which results in motor difficulties can cause writing by hand to be a problem, as can learning disabilities.

The diagnostic criteria of dyscalculia, as stipulated by the DSM-IV (APA 1994), states that writing skills are below what would be expected for the person's age, intelligence and education level. To receive a positive diagnosis, the difficulties have to be significant enough to cause an impact on academic or other areas of life.

In order to be eligible for additional support, educational or otherwise, an assessment may be required as proof of the level of need. If a person is intending to study and is aware that writing is a problem, an assessment or diagnosis can open the door to a wide range of support, including computer equipment, notetakers, extra time during exams and other support. Workplace support may also be required and should be provided by law.

Characteristics

The evidence for dysgraphia is seen in the written output of the person, although assessment must be made by an appropriate person as poor hand-writing may be an indicator of something else, or be an accurate reflection of a person's ability and education, which dysgraphic hand-writing is not. Observable characteristics may worsen at times of stress or when the person is expected to produce written work at speed:

- mixture of letter shapes and sizes – no consistency
- capitals and small letters used seemingly randomly
- mixture of printing and cursive writing
- unusual pen grip
- hand-writing difficult to read
- pain in hand during and after writing
- difficulty with other intricate motor tasks (shoe-laces, threading needle)
- difficulty in copying information accurately
- spontaneous written work may be particularly hard to read
- difficulty in keeping writing within required space or margins
- writing very slowly
- hand-writing slanted left and/or right across the page
- frustration at being unable to express thoughts.

Implications

Dysgraphia can result in associated difficulties of stress, frustration and low self-esteem as the person is unable to adequately express themselves in written form and perhaps does not achieve well academically due to the overwhelming focus on written work in most examination or accreditations systems. Some individuals with dysgraphia experience pain when writing and may also become tired easily at the effort of forming letters and controlling motor movements. Incorrect assumptions of low intelligence or laziness may be made when an individual is perceived to be able and yet cannot perform at the expected level.

Treatments and approaches

There is no one accepted method for supporting dysgraphia; again, as with dyscalculia, this information is largely repeated, although early intervention for children is advised. For those in adulthood, modification approaches may be too late to make a significant difference and management strategies may be more practical. For those seeking intervention, education specialists working within the area of learning difficulties, such as dyslexia and dyspraxia, will be able to provide specific strategies for support, which may help to address the root cause, rather than manage difficult situations. It is important for the person with dysgraphia to come to terms with the fact that they have many skills and abilities, but are disabled by society's focus on written measures as an assessment of ability and that if they can find strategies to minimize their difficulties, then perhaps they will feel less frustrated.

Self-help strategies

- Use a computer rather than pen and paper.

- Organize a notetaker or scribe for studying or taking exams (assessment may be required).

- Ask for extra time when taking exams (assessment may be required).

- Request an alternative assessment method to exam, such as presentation, video or portfolio of work (assessment may be required).

- Allow plenty of time for writing and take lots of breaks.

- If hands hurt when writing, rub them, shake them and give them a break.

- Use lined paper to give guidelines.

- Practise containing writing in defined spaces or boxes on the page.

- Minimize stress in other areas of life to avoid cumulative frustration around writing.

- Use a tape recorder to record yourself or draw pictures to express thoughts and feelings.

Supporting strategies

- Remember that dysgraphia must be supported under disability legislation and adjustments provided where required.

- Minimize the need for the person to copy written work from books or a whiteboard – provide them with notes when possible.

- Allow the person to use a Dictaphone or voice recorder to gather information, rather than taking written notes in meetings, lessons or other situations.

- Encourage the person to speak out loud when writing.

- Practise activities that involve fine motor skills – some individuals with dysgraphia have poor muscle tone, which may be improved through exercising.

- Understand that poor writing does not mean that the person is stupid or lazy.

- Encourage the drawing of pictures before writing to get visual reminders of what they want to express.

Words from those affected

Kit, who has dyspraxia and hand-writing difficulties, lists some of the related difficulties he has:

My main characteristics are a lack of coordination, poor organizational skills, poor and aversion to hand-writing, left and right confusions and executive memory. I'm rubbish at filling in forms and I'm a champion procrastinator. I left school at 13 because it went too slowly for me and I acted out a lot. I think other people could be a bit more open-minded and see someone who thinks or acts differently as intriguing rather than intimidating. Everyone is wired in different ways. If you want to group people with similarities, fair enough, but don't persecute them for it. If my brain didn't work this way I'd still have gifts and problems – they'd just be different.

CHAPTER 8

Tourette Syndrome

I'm a bit weird and a bit different and I don't give a damn. That makes me feel impressed with myself.

Introduction

Tourette syndrome – sometimes referred to as TS – is a neurological condition which causes 'tics'. These tics can be motor – physical body movements – and vocal – noises and words. They tend to be repetitive in nature and appear with no prior warning. The popular media portrayal of TS is of a person who shouts obscenities and insults, but this accounts for only a small proportion of the TS population. The degree to which a person is affected can vary widely from very minor twitching and blinking to whole body jerking movements and vocal shouting. Hence TS is part of what is known as 'tic spectrum disorder'. These are largely involuntary movements, which the person may be able to control, but only for a certain period of time, after which there is a need to release the build-up of tension involved from suppressing the tics. TS generally begins in childhood and the majority of people grow out of their tics or the tics become less visible or more controllable as people reach adulthood, particularly after adolescence and puberty.

For some adults, this is not the case and their tics persist, and sometimes worsen, throughout their life. While some people experience severe difficulty managing and living with TS and are keen to receive treatment and support to minimize its impact and presentation, there are others who feel that it is part of who they are and is a 'disability' only due to the intolerance of society.

History

Tourette syndrome was first identified as a medical phenomenon by Dr Georges Gilles de la Tourette (1857–1904), after whom the condition is now named. Gilles de la Tourette himself was an interesting character, whose work in the late nineteenth century focused on the use of new techniques of the time, including hypnotherapy and vibration. It is said that Sigmund Freud may have been influenced by Gilles de la Tourette's lectures on the subject, which he is reported to have attended. Gilles de la Tourette was a neuro-psychiatrist with a particular interest in 'hysteria' and was described as a very over-excitable man who led a colourful life. Only a few sketches and some incomplete biographical details remain about his life.

He first identified the characteristics of the condition which came to bear his name in 1884 and described these in nine patients who were exhibiting involuntary tics. The origin of this condition was thought to be psychiatric and some believed that the tics were the result of the repression of masturbation. 'Gilles de la Tourette' was used as a name for this new disorder and the subject was widely reported over the years until the condition lost the interest of physicians and largely disappeared from public knowledge.

Gilles de la Tourette himself in later life is said to have displayed both mania and depression and after losing his job due to his disturbed mental behaviour, he died in a mental hospital.

In the 1970s, Arthur and Elaine Shapiro changed the shape of Tourette syndrome and tic disorders by challenging the notion that they were psychological in nature and through their extensive work in this field for many years promoted the view, widely held today, that these are neurological in origin. Up until this time, tics had been treated by psychoanalysis, searching for the cause and the Shapiros' work criticized this means of intervention strongly, changing the treatment and understanding of Tourette syndrome.

Causes and current thinking

TS is a neurological condition which has a strong inherited component with a genetic origin. It is not a psychological condition, caused by stress or childhood emotional trauma as was originally thought, although some professionals still believe this to be the case. Researchers studying families have noted that parents and children share TS-type behaviours and there is said to be a 50 per cent chance of an identical twin having TS if their sibling has it (King and Leckman 2004, cited in Kutscher 2005). It is suggested that those with TS are more likely to have experienced a difficult birth, although this has not been studied sufficiently to fully support this idea. MRI (magnetic resonance imaging) scans of those with TS show small differences in the sizes of certain parts of the brain (Peterson 2001) and that the frontal lobe may be important in the ability to suppress tics. Other suggestions include dysfunction in dopamine production, although again the evidence is not conclusive.

TS is said to affect more males than females on a ratio of three or four to one (Kutscher 2005) and is also commonly seen in those with additional special needs and learning disabilities.

Research has suggested that tics tend to appear in clusters, with days in which they are worse than others, rather than uniformly over time, which leads to hypothesis involving neuronal firing patterns being a causal factor (Peterson and Leckman 1998).

There are no reliable figures for the prevalence of TS among adults, and due to the broad and varied nature of the spectrum, many adults may live without TS causing them significant difficulty; only a minority will be severely affected. Among children estimates of around 1 in 100 people experiencing TS are reported (Box 2008), but due to many people seeing a reduction of their tics after adolescence, adult numbers are likely to be much lower.

Diagnosis and assessment

TS is part of the spectrum of tic disorders which all have their own 'official' medical classification. Both the *Diagnostic and Statistical Manual of Mental Disorders* (APA 1994) and the *International Classification of Diseases* (ICD-10: WHO 1994) have their own diagnostic criteria, but some working in the field feel that these do not represent the reality of the presentation of tics in the population. Tic disorders can be broadly described as follows:

- Transient tic disorder: this is a short-term tic disorder which lasts between 4 weeks and 12 months and features more than one motor and/or vocal tic.

- Chronic tic disorder: this is described as one or more than one vocal or motor tics, but not both, which last for more than one year.

- Unspecified tic disorder: this describes the existence of one or more tics, but doesn't meet the criteria for a specified tic disorder.

- Tourette syndrome: the criterion for a diagnosis of TS requires that vocal and motor tics be present for more than one year.

A prerequisite of all tic disorders is that their onset was before the age of 18 years and that they are not due to any other condition or caused by medication.

Diagnosis is carried out by a doctor or other medical professional, preferably someone who has experience and can recognize a tic and rule out any other possible diagnosis. There are no tests or screening processes that can identify a tic disorder. A complete medical history should be taken to rule out prenatal trauma, childhood illness, accidents (particularly head injuries), drug use, medication or other conditions which might be the cause of the tics.

It should be noted that an adult may be very adept at repressing and hiding their tics and so either video evidence or accounts from family members may be required to provide a full picture of the extent of the tic behaviour.

It is useful to note that, like many neuro-diverse conditions, co-morbidity is the norm, rather than a rarity. Only 12 per cent of patients are reported to have tics alone (Box 2008), with the remainder having other conditions as well. These are most commonly reported to be attention deficit hyperactivity disorder (ADHD) and obsessive-compulsive disorder (OCD). Reported specific rates of co-morbidity between TS and other conditions vary hugely and are mostly generated from research on children, so true rates are not known. Leslie Packer (1998) introduced the term TS+ as a means of remembering that not all behaviours seen in these co-morbid individuals are attributable to TS, but may be caused by other condition(s) that they are affected by.

Other co-morbid conditions, which may affect those with TS, are anxiety and depression disorders. While not an integral part of TS, living life with tics and the negative reactions from others may increase the chances of these mood disorders. It is also important to note that stress does not cause tics; it may exacerbate the tendency to tic and increase their frequency and intensity, but it is not the cause. A significant number of people with TS are also thought to meet the criteria for ADHD.

Characteristics

There may be visible signs of TS, or there may be none. A person may be affected very mildly or they may have learned excellent techniques for suppressing or hiding their tics for long periods. The physical signs of TS are a number of physical and oral tics, which will vary in type, frequency and severity. The one consistent thing about tics is their inconsistency. The desire to perform a tic is described as being like suppressing the urge to sneeze (Box 2008) – successfully held off for a short period, but in the end usually has to be let out. The sensory feelings prior to a person releasing a tic have been described as 'urges' and people with TS report a feeling that things are 'not quite right' before performing a tic (Packer 1998). To describe the tics as involuntary is not entirely correct for most people with TS, who feel that they have some element of control, but the need to tic can be overwhelming if suppressed for too long and not be under the person's control any longer. Commonly, someone who has suppressed their tics throughout the day at school or work may return home (to a safe environment) and 'explode in tics' (Packer 1998). It is not a worsening of the tics due to the anxiety involved in the suppression, just a release of a build-up of tics. Tics can appear more often when the person is stressed or inactive. Being focused on an activity, playing sport or other task seems to reduce the likelihood of tics in some people.

The features of the tic could be almost any kind of motor or vocal behaviour imaginable. Examples of tics that may be seen could include the following:

- Simple physical or 'motor' tics:
  - blinking the eyes

- rolling the head
- shrugging the shoulders
- twitching the nose
- opening the mouth
- tossing the hair
- Complex repetitive movements involving several muscle groups, such as:
  - twisting the body
  - pulling clothes
  - smelling objects
  - hitting self or others
  - tensing muscle groups
  - jumping or hopping
  - flapping arms
- Vocal tics:
  - coughing
  - sniffing
  - clearing the throat
  - grunting
  - repeating whole words or phrases – echophenomena
  - spitting
  - laughing.

Media interest has focused on 'corprolalia', which is the shouting of obscenities and socially inappropriate remarks, such as name-calling, or behaving inappropriately, such as doing things they shouldn't. Only a very small minority of those with TS are affected in this way. It should be noted that the key feature of corprolalia is its random nature with words often being said in the middle of a sentence, as opposed to someone simply cursing for a valid reason. A person may call a passer-by a name relating to their physical appearance – 'fat pig'. The person with corprolalia is unable to suppress these comments, which causes extreme stress and embarrassment for them and other people. A feature of TS is 'copropraxia' with which a person will make rude physical gestures. For those affected, there is often a significant, negative impact on their lives and how they are perceived and treated by other people, who are unaware of their condition.

Implications

The main difficulties faced by those with TS are the reactions of others in society to their 'inappropriate' behaviours. This can cause low self-esteem and confidence and result in people with TS choosing not to meet new people and finding it difficult to form personal relationships. It can be hard to keep track of conversations or instructions as tics, or the suppression of them, can intrude on the person's thoughts. They may avoid situations where they cannot mask or manage the tic and therefore become socially isolated. TS may also go undiagnosed due to a lack of knowledge by medical professionals, who may try to attribute the tics to another cause (typically psychological). In terms of safety, TS may affect the individual's ability to drive, swim or take part in other activities where motor control is a necessity.

Anecdotal reports from some people with TS report that they cannot work or study as their tics are so big and frequent that it makes learning or working impossible. This, of course, leads on to occupational and economic implications throughout the person's life, who may not be able to reach their academic potential and feel frustrated and also have to live on a low income.

Additional issues may be that the person physically harms themselves as a result of their tics – repeatedly hitting themselves, or damaging muscles from violent thrusts and spasms.

Treatments and approaches

Some people with TS are treated with medication, specifically those which affect dopamine production. There are a whole range of prescribed medications depending on the view of the medical professional and any additional co-morbidity exhibited by the patient. Medication for ADHD, OCD, depression and anxiety is widely used and may have a positive or negative affect on the tics. It is important to monitor closely the effects of any medication and adjust as necessary. Behavioural therapy is also used, particularly a programme called 'habit reversal therapy', which uses a range of techniques including relaxation and the learning of new responses to the urge to tic. The success rate of any intervention varies widely from person to person and there is certainly no conclusive evidence of any particular treatment or medication which has across the board high success rates. Counselling and other psychological approaches may be beneficial for managing the stress, anxiety or depression often experienced by those with TS, which may in turn enable increased manageability of the tics.

Strategies for supporting individuals

Some people learn to hide their tics very successfully by incorporating them into their normal actions, such as telling people they have a cold if they sniff or reaching for something when a motor tic displays itself. It can be an exhausting process to manage life in this way. Swedish singer-songwriter Jonas Altberg, otherwise known as Basshunter, has spoken openly about his TS and how he has learned to successfully suppress his tics to the point that no one would know he is affected. Other people do not wish to conceal their tics and feel that society needs to be more accepting of diversity.

TS is a disability, which requires support and adjustments to be made by law, and therefore no young person or adult should be treated unfavourably as a result of their tics. The reality is that often lack of understanding and awareness do lead to difficulties in school, college or the workplace. If a person with TS is experiencing these issues, they should seek request training for colleagues and possibly adjustments to be made to enable them to carry out their duties. These adjustments may include delegating certain tasks – for someone with TS who has vocal tics, this could include not being asked to make phone calls to customers or for someone with motor tics, some elements of manual handling may be dangerous. It also may involve alterations to working hours, the workplace environment and communication methods. These adjustments would be made in consultation with the individual and the employer.

Self-help strategies

- Learn about your tics and what triggers them. If you are aware of your tics, keep a diary to see if you can spot any patterns or associated factors. Knowing when they are likely to be more prevalent will help you to plan strategies in advance to minimize them.

- Remember that TS may be affected by stress for some people, so taking exercise and learning relaxation and stress management techniques may minimize tics. The more you worry about your tics, the more likely they are to occur.

- Be aware that the challenge of living with TS can cause psychological difficulties, so seeking counselling to work through these aspects and learn to feel positive about your TS can be helpful.

- Acknowledge that being on the receiving end of stares and comments can take its toll on self-esteem. Learning self-acceptance will be of real benefit.

Supporting strategies

- Learn as much as you can about TS, so you can understand and also educate others who may not be supportive.

- Understand that if you are working or living with someone with TS, it is important to find out how they wish you to behave around them. Ask them what they would like from you.

- Remember that some people would like to be asked about their tics, or feel quite comfortable making jokes about them.

- Be aware that some people prefer that their tics are simply ignored and not mentioned. Take a lead from others who know the person, if you can.

- Ask the person with TS how they feel when the tics occur (if you know that they wish to talk about it) and you will get a better sense of their perspective and be able to react accordingly.

- Do not ask someone to stop performing tics: this is not helpful, because if they could, they would have done so already.

- Appreciate that your own embarrassment or discomfort may make the person with TS feel worse about their tics. Be aware of your own feelings and thoughts about TS.

- Recognize when the person may need your support in a situation and when they prefer to manage it themselves. Do not automatically take over to avoid discomfort, as this may make the person feel inadequate.

- Remember that being positive to a person with TS and helping them to see that they are more than just their tics – that you value them as a person – will help to raise their self-esteem and confidence.

Words from those affected

Russ, an adult with TS, describes how it affects him:

My TS became apparent when I was around the age of 10 or 11. I had a variety of tics throughout my teenage years, mostly facial tics. I now have a core of three or four tics with the odd new one turning up now and again. My main tics are small sudden jerks of the head; rapid, tight blinking of my eyes and nose twitching. Sometimes I will tense up my stomach muscles rapidly, which makes my whole body shake as though I am coughing silently. I can't think of an hour going by without a tic. It feels like an unsuppressible urge to do something stupid and a compulsion to do negative things. The more conscious I am of the tics, the harder it is to suppress them. Being active and preoccupied definitely reduced the frequency of my tics – anything which requires a lot of focus, such as sport, really helps. When I am winding down or driving, for example, my mind is not occupied and the tics become more frequent, which makes it hard to relax. They don't tend to be more prominent in stressful situations, but definitely do so during stressful periods in my life. I was very conscious of them when

I was younger, particularly in evaluation situations, such as meeting girls, but as I have got older I care a lot less.

Personally, I can't say that any of my tics prevent me from doing what other people do and I work in management consultancy, which requires me to regularly be in evaluation scenarios, such as giving presentations. I don't tend to tell people I meet that I have TS and I would prefer it if people just ignored it, rather than asked me about it, but that's just me.

CHAPTER 9

Anxiety Disorders

I get annoyed at myself when I start to panic over something stupid like going through a tunnel. I know it's irrational and that I'm not in any danger, but I can't seem to stop my body from going into a state of panic.

Introduction

All of us get anxious from time to time. Worrying and anxiety are a normal and useful part of life. They give us signals to tell us when something is not right or when we need to take extra care to ensure our safety or a particular outcome to a situation. For those with anxiety disorders, anxiety is not part of life; it has taken over life.

Someone may be considered to have an anxiety disorder when their worries and anxiety of both the present and the future prevent them from enjoying normal daily life. The person may struggle to control their thoughts and feel that worries are constantly going round in their head and they are unable to get rid of them. An anxiety disorder results in worries about things that don't really need to be worried about, or things that are very unlikely to happen at all. The anxiety for the person with an anxiety disorder has reached a point where it is no longer a useful indicator of danger or concern, but is triggered by any minor event or thought to the point where is disables the person and impact on their life in a significant way. Someone with an anxiety disorder is likely to avoid situations, people and places that cause them anxiety. They may suffer from insomnia, mood swings and low self-esteem. Often people are aware that their worries and anxiety are not helpful, but struggle to put them in perspective in order to move on with their lives.

History

Mentions of anxiety and panic have been made since early records began. Early fears and anxious states were attributed to demons, deities and other spirits, or to individual sin or inherent weakness of character (Anderson 2009). As long ago as the 1900s, researchers were blaming the stresses of modern life on increasing anxiety among people, with cities and working areas yielding high numbers of people with mental health issues (Porter 1997). Large amounts of research have been carried out over the years, with genetic factors being identified in the 1980s, offering a new perspective from the general thinking that mental illness was due to purely psychological or stress-related factors. This discovery testified to at least some inherent brain difference in families where this predisposition was evident (Shorter 1997). Subsequent studies and developments on the chemical make-up of the brain and the effect of medication and therapeutic techniques, such as cognitive behavioural therapy, have advanced understanding and treatment of anxiety disorders.

Causes and current thinking

As with most of the conditions in this book, conclusive evidence as to causes is not clear and often much debated. Certain areas of the brain are implicated, particularly the amygdala, which concerns balance (Balaban and Thayer 2001). Levels of neurotransmitters may be different in those with anxiety, but whether this is a cause of or the result of the anxiety disorder is not fully known. There does appear to be familial tendencies towards anxiety disorders with several members of the same family likely to be affected. This may be due to a genetic predisposition which is triggered by external events in the person's life. Stress and other factors can increase the chance of being affected by an anxiety disorder and often the onset of an anxiety disorder is after a major or traumatic life event. The characteristics and severity may worsen at subsequent stressful time in the person's life and they may always be especially susceptible to anxiety and worry.

Anxiety disorders is an umbrella term which encompasses a range of conditions, including OCD, phobias, social anxiety disorder, agoraphobia and panic disorder. It is not known why different people experience different types of anxiety disorder. This may be due to childhood experiences and traumas or personality type.

It is estimated that between 2 and 5 per cent of adults experience anxiety disorders at some point in their lives (Hale 1997). Anxiety is seen more commonly in women than men (Hale 1997). Panic disorders are seen in 0.7 per cent of the population and are even spread across men and women (Office for National Statistics 2000). Unlike most of the other conditions in this book, anxiety disorders can appear and disappear throughout life, but it seems that the tendency to be affected is higher in certain people and that the ability of the person to maintain their anxiety at a manageable level is crucial in whether a disorder will be diagnosed or not. Many people may slip in and out of diagnosable anxiety levels throughout their lives and, as stated above, many people will never seek any help.

Anxiety is experienced by many people affected by neurodiversity as they often have difficulty 'fitting in' with others due to their different information processing mechanisms and different social understanding. For a person who exists in a world in which they feel frequently confused and out of control, anxiety is a natural by-product. Although it is not specified as an essential criterion for any of the other conditions mentioned in this book, it is highly likely to be experienced. Tony Attwood suggests that over half of adolescents with Asperger syndrome have a secondary anxiety disorder (Attwood 2006). In the USA, a national ADHD prevalence and co-morbidity study found around 47 per cent of people had both ADHD and anxiety disorders. Some 88 per cent of people with Tourette syndrome experience ADHD or anxiety disorders as well as their TS (Tourettes Action 2009).

High levels of anxiety are also experienced by those with alcohol or drug use problems. These substances are often used initially as self-medication for anxiety (Mental Health Foundation 2006), but go on to create increased anxiety levels as a result of continued consumption. Treatment for alcoholism or drug use that doesn't address the underlying anxiety which led to the problem is likely to fail. Anxiety will increase as a result of withdrawal and then as the person experiences life as an anxious person who has had their only coping strategy removed (Tinsley and Hendrickx 2008).

Diagnosis and assessment

Anxiety disorders are usually diagnosed by a GP or other medical practitioner through observation and questioning of the individual. The diagnosis is a subjective one as there is no test for anxiety and the diagnosis given may vary depending on the practitioner consulted. There are criteria for different anxiety disorders to differentiate between them. These are summarized for some of the most common anxiety disorders below.

Generalized anxiety disorder (GAD)

Generalized anxiety disorder is characterized by non-specific worry, that is worry that is not isolated to one topic or situation, but is present for a significant part of the person's life over a given period.

Features of the diagnostic criteria include:

- Excessive worry and anxiety which is difficult to control.

- At least three of the following associated symptoms must be present:

  o   tires easily

  o   short-tempered

  o   difficulty concentrating

  o   tension (may result in headaches or muscle pain)

  o   nausea and/or vomiting

  o   difficulty relaxing – feeling on edge.

- The cause of focus of the anxiety is not caused by another anxiety disorder, other psychological condition or by medication, drugs or alcohol.

- Characteristics must have been present for at least six months.

- The anxiety must be at a level to cause significant difficulties in functioning.

Social anxiety disorder (SAD)

Social anxiety disorder is a fear and sometimes avoidance of situations involving people and social situations. The person may become highly anxious at the thought of forthcoming events.

Social anxiety may be particularly prevalent in those with Asperger syndrome, who experience difficulties understanding social interaction. The diagnostic criteria for social anxiety disorder state that a diagnosis should not be made if another pervasive developmental disorder (such as Asperger syndrome) is present (Ghaziuddin 2005). This assumes that the criteria for SAD are encompassed into conditions like Asperger syndrome.

Features include the following:

- Fear or anxiety in relation to people; being near, or having to interact with, others.

- Fear of judgement or criticism by other people, which may result in being hypersensitive to comment from others.

- Dread or panic before certain situations, and potential replaying or ruminating on the event afterwards.

- Physical symptoms such as shaking, nausea and raised heart rate.

- The characteristics must be present for at least six months.

Specific phobias

A phobia is a fear of a specific thing or situation that is excessive or irrational. The phobia tends to be quite easy to identify and most people are aware of their own phobias. The phobia can be about almost anything. More common phobias include spiders, heights, flying and the dark. More unusual phobias, but which can be equally debilitating, include beards, words, flutes and empty rooms. The level at which a person is affected varies from those who can be in the presence of the feared object to those who enter a state of panic at the thought of it, hearing someone else speak about it or seeing a picture of the object. If the phobia is extreme, the person may avoid situations where exposure to the object of the phobia is possible. A phobia is not simply a dislike of something; distress is experienced to a degree where normal functioning is not possible and panic is present.

Diagnostic features of phobias include the following:

- Persistent or excessive fear of a specific object or situation. Fear may be triggered by thoughts or images of the object or situation rather than just the physical experience.

- Anxiety response and panic state are triggered by exposure to the object or situation.

- The person has some understanding that the fear and response is excessive, but is unable to control this.

- The situation may be avoided or suffered with great distress and anxiety.

- The phobia results in significant impairment to functioning and/or distress and anxiety levels.

- The characteristics are not better described by another anxiety disorder or condition and are not the result of medication or drug use.

Panic disorder

A panic attack is a common feature of many anxiety disorders and is described as a physical state of heightened anxiety complete with physical symptoms, which may include:

- raised heart rate

- feeling faint

- shortness of breath

- flushed face

- sweating

- shaking
- chest pain
- fear of losing control and becoming hysterical.

Panic disorder is described when there is no immediate or obviously attributable cause for the panic attack; it just comes out of the blue. People who suffer from panic attacks often fear that they are going to die and become afraid that they will have more attacks. This can lead to avoidance of situations which may trigger an attack. A diagnosis of panic disorder is made if the condition is not better described as another anxiety disorder and the attacks are unexpected, i.e. not triggered by a phobia or social situation.

Agoraphobia

Agoraphobia is not, as used to be commonly believed, a fear of open space. It usually manifests as a fear of not being in control. The person may have an intense fear of being away from the safety of home, being in places where immediate escape is not possible (tunnels, lifts, crowded places, bridges, buses or trains) or being alone. There is often a fear of having a panic attack in such a situation and thus a fear of losing control or humiliating oneself. These situations may then be avoided to prevent this from occurring. The person may find themselves restricted to 'safe' places and severely limit their ability to cope with daily living.

Characteristics

Many people become very effective in hiding their anxiety disorders as they are aware that their behaviour is excessive or irrational and do not want to look 'crazy' or foolish in front of others. It is only when one person in a group discloses that they have an anxiety disorder than others suddenly open up and do the same. It can be amazing to learn how many people experience these difficulties and they are often those who appear most confident and composed. Appearances can be very deceptive. The physical indicators of a panic attack are the most likely seen characteristics of an anxiety disorder, although again these can be very well concealed. A flushed face, rapid speech or total silence and agitated behaviour are often signs that someone is experiencing mental distress.

Generalized anxiety disorder

A person with GAD is likely to be anxious and tense for quite a lot of the time. They may have trouble getting to sleep and generally worry a lot about things that may be perceived as not being that important.

Social anxiety disorder

Social situations or the anticipation of social situations will be the trigger for anxiety for a person with SAD. An avoidance of public speaking, eating and drinking in front of people or even attending an event where lots of people will be present are likely visible characteristics. A person with SAD may be hypersensitive to the opinions and criticism of others and may seek reassurance about themselves and their behaviour. They may lead quite an isolated existence and not have many friends and social contacts as they may be unable to cope with going out and socializing. Someone with SAD may come across as quite a nervous, shy or unconfident person.

Specific phobias

Most adults with phobias know they have one and know what it is that they are afraid of. This is useful as it means that often they will tell you what it is if a trigger situation is due to occur. If the trigger is unexpected, it is quite common for someone to say, 'Sorry, I have got a real phobia about … I need to get out of here'. A person in a zoo insect house with a phobia of bugs is easy to spot: it is the person edging round the far side of the room, shoulders hunched and tense, wide, panic-stricken eyes and sweat glistening from their forehead. These are very specific and probably easy to spot as the person will behave markedly differently than they do at any other time.

Panic disorder

As described in many of the above paragraphs, panic disorder is indicated by a panic attack, the most obvious and visible sign of any anxiety disorder. It may come on unannounced with no trig-gering event, unlike with a phobia, and may be in the middle of the night or during an otherwise relaxing situation, so may be a bit of a surprise. Sometimes people having panic attacks struggle to breathe and feel tightness in their chests, which they fear signifies a heart attack. This makes them panic even more. People do not die from panic attacks, although it can feel that way at the time. Characteristically, someone experiencing a panic attack is a very frightened person at that time.

Agoraphobia

An agoraphobic person is likely to show a preference for environ-ments and situations that they can control and in which they feel safe. They may avoid travelling, going on holiday, leaving home, visiting new places, or crowds. If they do engage in these activities, it may be done with a large amount of distress and anxiety, which can result in exhaustion and stress. The anticipation of unpredictable events and possible triggers can cause panic attacks and distress as well as the actual event itself.

Implications

Anxiety disorders are invisible disabilities, which are often greatly misunderstood. They can seriously control a person's life with unwanted and irrational thoughts, behaviours and fears. The person may avoid many situations to try to prevent the onset of anxiety or a panic attack and then become fearful of the possibility of future anxiety and so then avoid more situations to ensure this doesn't happen. This then becomes a vicious, downward spiral of avoidance and fear. First comes fear of the situation and then fear of the anxiety. For those severely affected, study, work and personal relationships become very difficult or even impossible, if travel, social situations or the need to carry out compulsions are a requirement.

Treatments and approaches

Anxiety disorders are categorized as mental health issues and access to statutory support is usually through your GP. Often services are heavily subscribed and it may take some time for a referral appointment to a specialist mental health practitioner. The alternative is to find a private therapist or practitioner and pay for their services. There are many different treatments and therapies which can help different types of anxiety and it may take some time before you find one which suits your needs.

Medication

Medication is widely prescribed for anxiety disorders and there is a vast range of drugs available. These can be tolerated differently from person to person so it may be necessary to try a few different ones before you find one which helps. Anxiety UK has a comprehensive list of the most commonly prescribed medication for anxiety disorders on its website (www.anxietyuk.org.uk).

Psychological therapies

Counselling, hypnotherapy, cognitive behavioural therapy and other therapies are said to be very effective in helping people overcome their anxiety. These may have to be paid for privately as funded provision is limited and over-stretched. Cognitive behavioural therapy can be very helpful in challenging distorted thinking and helping you to see what is real and how to work through panic and anxiety when they become overwhelming. This involves self-talking to work through what is really happening, rather than what you think is happening.

Self-help strategies

- Read and learn about how anxiety works and affects you; this can be a powerful means of overcoming it. There are many books available on managing anxiety and using cognitive behavioural techniques to change thoughts and the meanings attributed to them.

- Join a self-help group, which involves meeting others and sharing your experiences. This can reduce feelings of isolation and that you are the only person going through this. Other people may have valuable experiences and strategies to share and sometimes just talking to people who understand can be really reassuring.

- Get help and/or medication if you need it. Don't be afraid to ask for help. You don't have to suffer alone.

- Use cognitive behavioural type methods to work through irrational thoughts and worries.

- Remember that just because you have a thought doesn't mean you have to listen to it or act upon it – it may be distorted. Learn techniques to identify unhelpful thought patterns.

- Realize that you are not alone or going mad. Many people experience anxiety and it is a normal part of everyday life. Remembering this can help to put your feelings in perspective. Anxiety is often invisible and you cannot tell who is feeling it – often the calmest looking people may be the most terrified!

- Believe that there is life beyond anxiety and that you can beat it. Find personal accounts and inspiring stories of people who have battled anxiety and overcome it.

Supporting strategies

- Take the person's concerns seriously; do not tell them they are stupid to be afraid, even if you don't understand.

- Ask the person what they would like you to do if they become anxious; some people would like help, others prefer for it to be ignored.

- Find out about the many self-help books, websites and forums that are available. Educate yourself and encourage the person to find others like them and find out how to deal with it.

- Encourage the person to accept themselves exactly as they are.

- Support the person in learning to laugh at themselves and some of their strange ways. This can be very empowering and increase confidence if it is understood that they are loved and liked just the same.

- Remember that panic attacks do not cause heart attacks.

- Ask the person: How many of the things that you fear have ever actually happened?

- Try to get the person to worry about things when they actually happened, not in case they do.

Words from those affected

Gloria, a woman in her forties, explains the onset of agoraphobia in adulthood:

My panic attacks began when I was 33. I had a very traumatic period where my mother died, my marriage broke down and I lost my home. I always felt that it was like my brain had said: 'That's it, I can't take any more.' Like I had reached the limits of the amount of stress I could cope with and that I had no control at all over my life as I hadn't been able to stop all of the horrible things that had happened. I found myself terrified of buses, lifts, cinemas, corridors, tunnels – anywhere that I felt I couldn't immediately get out of. It was very strange at first as I had never felt like that before and I was annoyed at myself for getting in such a state when everyone else around me was fine. These feelings have not gone away in eight years, although they come and go over periods of time. Sometimes I feel quite calm and relaxed about certain situations and then suddenly the same thing will cause me huge panic for a few weeks, before it abates again. There was a period when I couldn't get on a plane without medication, but I can do so sometimes now, although I will avoid underground trains at all costs and find being on one exhausting as the physical toll of a panic attack is so big. I had a period of being afraid I would be sick on trains and planes so I would make myself throw up before I got on to make sure there was nothing left in my stomach. This seems to have pretty much stopped – for now. I find being alone very frightening at times as I think of all the terrible things that could happen to me. I am afraid of strangers coming and attacking me. I don't know why, just a feeling that I wouldn't be able to control that sort of situation. I think I see myself as helpless due to the things that happened eight years ago, which I couldn't prevent and so I assume I am powerless. When I am in a panic-inducing situation, I distract myself by listening to music, reading or talking to someone and I find that really helps. The more I worry about having a panic attack, the worse it is. I hate anyone asking me how I'm feeling if they know it is a difficult situation for me, as this makes me think about it myself and will start me panicking. I would rather they just talked normally to me and not made a big deal. Not many people know how badly this affects me. People think I am a confident and capable person, which I am in many situations, but in other situations, where most people wouldn't even bat an eyelid, I suffer horribly. In some ways, I think I am a stronger person because of my anxiety; I am too stubborn to miss out on things because of a stupid, irrational glitch in my head, so I force myself to do things even though it is a real struggle, and then I'm quite proud of myself for having done it. I feel like it's a battle and I'm not one for giving up the fight.

CHAPTER 10

Obsessive-Compulsive Disorder (OCD)

People should act as they would normally towards me. OCD is not easy, but the most effective way of maintaining yourself in society and the real world is by being treated the same as everyone else.

Introduction

Obsessive-compulsive disorder (OCD) is a type of anxiety disorder, but as it appears to accompany many of the conditions covered in this book to a higher degree than would be expected by chance (particularly Asperger syndrome, Tourette syndrome and ADHD, all conditions that affect the frontal cortex of the brain), it should be covered in more detail than other specific anxiety disorders, and so deserves it own chapter. Those who are affected by OCD typically feel compelled to carry out repetitive behaviours or thoughts in order to diminish extreme feelings of anxiety. A person may have a dread of dying from infection and believe that everything they touch may harm them and thus either avoid touching anything, or wash their hands repetitively and very frequently in order to reduce this possibility. Those with OCD appear to be convinced that their safety, and that of others around them, is dependent on the correct performance of ritualistic thoughts and behaviours – which may have no rational connection to the fear. A person may believe that saying a certain word a certain number of times will protect them from danger and harm. Some OCD behaviour appears irrational and bizarre, but to the person affected, the fear of not carrying out the behaviour is so great, that their rational logic (which often knows that the behaviour makes no sense) is overridden.

History

Early reports of OCD type behaviour have been documented since the seventeenth century, where reports were made of individuals at religious services being afraid of uttering obscenities and so needing to remain silent. Esquirol (1838) called OCD a form of partial insanity or monomania. After this monomania idea had been discarded in the 1850s, obsessions and compulsions were seen to exist as part of the anxiety disorders spectrum, which includes panic disorders and phobias.

Causes and current thinking

The prevalence of OCD is reported to be around 1–3 per cent of the population, although this is likely to be an underestimate as many people do not seek treatment (Fireman *et al.* 2001). The background information to anxiety disorders in Chapter 9 applies to OCD. Recent studies of children with OCD (Dare *et al.* 2005) have made links to potential bacterial causes, which may affect autoimmune responses and could provide new insight into the origin of OCD. General research and findings into anxiety disorders is equally applicable to OCD, as there is a considerable overlap between other anxiety disorders and causal factors.

Diagnosis and assessment

Diagnosis can be carried out by a medical professional, preferably one with experience of anxiety disorders, and particularly of OCD. OCD is a debilitating condition which affects the person's ability to get on with their lives. OCD generally begins to affect people in adolescence or their early twenties, but OCD-UK reports that it may take some people 10–15 years to seek help (OCD-UK 2009). This should be taken into account when someone seeks diagnosis, as it may have taken many years for them to gain the courage to seek help. It is important, therefore, not to trivialize their concerns, or make the assumption that because they have managed for so long without support, that they are not significantly affected by their OCD.

OCD is characterized by intrusive and repetitive thoughts, impulses and images which the person finds difficult to control or ignore. This is the obsessive part of OCD. These cause the person to (usually) feel compelled to carry out rituals and repetitive or avoidance behaviours to somehow protect the person from the perceived danger of the obsessions. There is generally an awareness that the thoughts and behaviours are irrational, but the person is usually unable to stop doing them for fear of something terrible happening. OCD is time-consuming and exhausting for the person and also very difficult for family members, who may find it hard to understand why the person is locked in this irrational world. As with other anxiety disorders, a degree of concern about double checking that the cooker (stove) is switched off or not stepping on the cracks in the pavement (sidewalk) are all part of human quirks and behaviour. Here are some examples of OCD:

- A person who believes that if they do not touch a certain piece of clothing a certain number of times, then terrible harm will come to a loved one.

- Someone who, even though they are sure they checked that the taps (faucets) were turned off before they left home, becomes increasingly convinced that they didn't and the house will flood. They may even return home in order to check if they are unable to rid themselves of the thought.

- A person who has violent thoughts about harming other people by driving their car into them and becomes convinced that they will act upon those thoughts. They may avoid driving or travelling in cars as they fear they will not be able to stop themselves from doing something harmful.

The criteria for OCD encompass both obsessions and compulsions.

Obsessions

- The person has persistent and recurring impulses, thoughts or images that cause distress or anxiety and are not within the realms of reasonable concern or worry.

- Attempts are made to suppress or ignore the obsessive thoughts, or to combat them by avoidance, ritual or other thoughts.

- There is a recognition that the obsessive thoughts are not based in reality, but are in the person's imagination.

Compulsions

- There are repetitive physical behaviours, ritual or mental thoughts that the person feels compelled to carry out in accordance with rules devised by the person themselves.

- The behaviours are carried out to prevent or reduce anxiety caused by some perceived danger or situation. The behaviours are not connected to the issue and so can have no impact on the outcome, or are executed to a degree in excess of that generally considered necessary to the situation.

- Compulsions can be overt – checking, washing, touching (number of times, or same number with each hand or foot, etc.).

- Compulsions can be covert – mental actions, rather than physical, which means they are often hidden (counting, repeating words in head, changing distressing images for different ones).

- Obsessions and compulsions take up more than one hour per day.

- The person must realize, at some point, that the behaviour or thoughts are not rational.

Characteristics

Although many people with OCD are very adept at hiding their compulsions, these are perhaps the most likely to be visible to the observer. OCD can be very debilitating and affect a person's work and personal life. It can make a person very anxious, particularly if they feel they have been unable to carry out their compulsive behaviours, at which time they may fear that a disastrous outcome is inevitable. OCD-UK has produced an information booklet on OCD, which outlines the following characteristics:

For someone who fears contamination or germs, there may be avoidance of:

- shaking hands

- touching door handles

- using public toilets (bathrooms)

- eating food that they have not prepared themselves

- washing hands excessively.

Compulsions can involve repeated checking of certain things. These can be carried out in a specific ritualistic way and may be done several times before the person is satisfied and can move on. The person seems to demonstrate a lack of confidence in themselves that they are capable of doing something correctly the first time and also a worry that something bad will happen if they have forgotten, which they will be responsible for. They may ask for reassurance from others that they have done the task. Observable checking behaviours may include:

- cooker (stove) knobs

- doors being shut properly

- light switches

- taps (faucets)

- keys

- items in handbag (purse)

- contents of letters before sealing.

Other compulsions may be:

- having a fear of sexually abusing children or loved ones

- wanting to have sex with someone other than one's partner

- thinking that colours or numbers can bring good or bad luck

- believing that thoughts can cause bad things to happen

- feeling that whatever thoughts the person has can come true so they are responsible for outcome

- having religious beliefs, sinful thoughts and fear of recrimination

- being afraid of violently harming other people

- acting on unwanted impulses – fear of crashing car into someone, pushing someone in front of a train, killing children

- counting repeatedly – patterns on wall, items on shelf

- rereading a letter over and over again before sending

- needing orderliness and perfection – spending time on lining things up and cleaning

- hoarding – buying more than one needs 'just in case' they run out

- being unable to throw anything away – may feel bad things will happen if do so.

Implications

OCD can be a very debilitating condition, which completely controls a person's life. The World Health Organization ranks OCD as the tenth most disabling illness of any kind (OCD-UK 2009). This is an exhausting existence involving repetitive rituals, routines and ruminations. As with all anxiety disorders, OCD can restrict normal functioning severely and prevent study, work and personal relationships. People with OCD often feel that they are going mad and cannot control their behaviour; the compulsion to perform the ritual is so strong. A lack of understanding from others can also make life difficult, if they are not supported.

Treatments and approaches

There are a number of strategies and treatments to overcome OCD, although many people continue to be affected to some degree even following treatment. Medication, self-help techniques and cognitive behavioural therapy are the most widely known forms of support. Self-knowledge and learning about one's own OCD can be a very powerful tool in reducing the control it has over the person's mind and life. Medication can be helpful in reducing general anxiety. A wide variety of anti-anxiety medication is available and the suitability of any particular form will depend on the individual and how they are affected. Cognitive behavioural therapy is a very practical form of talking therapy which focuses on unhelpful thoughts and beliefs and challenges them, creating new thought patterns and ways of behaving which are more functional. These tools can be learned and then applied to new situations which cause stress and anxiety.

Self-help strategies

- Think about cognitive behavioural therapy (CBT), which is very helpful in the treatment of OCD – either through a therapist, or by reading books and using techniques. See Further Reading section for books on CBT.

- Take each day at a time and praise yourself for each small success.

- Try to reduce rituals and checking gradually, rather than all at once. If you usually check 20 times per hour, try checking only 18 times and then reduce the number.

- Don't give up if you can't manage to reach your goal – just start again and keep trying.

- Realize that obsessions and compulsions make you a prisoner. They do not keep you safe.

- Think through each of your rituals and ask yourself: Why do I do this? How does doing this keep me safe? What would happen if I didn't do it? It may take time, but challenging your thoughts and belief will help to weaken them.

- Talk to others with OCD and find out what works for them.

- Learn to laugh at yourself and some of your strange behaviours: it will weaken their control over you.

Supporting strategies

- Remember that unconditional acceptance is a good first step in supporting someone with OCD. Accept that the person's reality is very frightening and that they are not 'crazy' or 'mad'.

- Realize that besides the strategies outlined in Chapter 9 on anxiety disorders, care should be taken when challenging or supporting someone with OCD. If their condition is not fully understood, the person may suffer more stress from 'helpful' people than without.

- Understand that even though the behaviour of a person with OCD may appear irrational, it is rooted in meeting a need that the person has for security, control and safety.

- Do not ask someone to 'just stop' performing their rituals. If they could do it that easily, they would.

- Acknowledge that treatment is likely to be required for OCD and the person should be supported and encouraged to seek the help they need.

Words from those affected

Rachael, a young woman who has been affected by obsessive-compulsive disorder since early childhood, explains how her rituals are part of her life:

The main characteristics of my condition are counting, ordering, checking and especially symmetry. I have obsessions surrounding perfectionism, including things needing to be logical and 'right'. My OCD is part of my personality, as I've had it since the age of seven years and it is part of how I have developed as a person.

I feel my condition has given me depth of character, as I understand how much of a struggle can be caused by your own mind. I have experienced feeling so trapped and low that I could not even function to speak or move some days, during my childhood and teenage years.

As I found socializing difficult as a child and teenager, due to OCD and subsequent internal and external aggression, I am still learning how to socialize effectively now. Some aspects of socializing, such as eating and getting ready to leave the house to go out, can be challenging. My gulps of drink and mouthfuls of food when eating and drinking are counted, to ensure even numbers of food mouthfuls and odd gulps of drink are consumed. I get round this by counting in small numbers so I don't have to remember exact numbers. However, I am very open about letting my friends know about my condition, to which most people have been inquisitive and open to understanding. My friends don't define me by my condition, but they do sometimes joke about my rituals with me in a positive way, as do my family.

I struggled and under-achieved at school and college, due to my condition causing me to find reading and writing difficult. I have rituals whereby I have to blink at certain parts of a word and frequently count words in sentences and paragraphs, ensuring I keep counting until the full sentences come to an even number. Also, when writing, the ink has to join together completely in each word, if not I will repeatedly write over the gap with my pen touching the paper until the gap is filled with the number of touches ending in an odd number. These rituals have continued into my adult life; I have since successfully completed a college course and degree, though these were extremely challenging.

When I walk, if one foot touches a crack in the pavement, the other foot must touch another crack in the same place on my foot. This means that my walk can look somewhat ridiculous at times, though thankfully I can ignore it sometimes. I have learned to appreciate how funny I look when doing this unusual walk and laugh to myself as I move along, which I'm sure makes me appear even stranger, but I would rather this than make myself unwell through anxiety.

Every movement, thought and action still involves OCD, to a greater or lesser extent, such as my facial tics and movements which I do throughout my waking hours to maintain symmetry in my body. I am continually correcting my body and the placing of objects around me, while often counting people and things and checking that I really did put my purse (wallet) in my bag (purse), even though I checked 13 times already.

People should act as they would normally towards me. OCD is not easy, but the most effective way of maintaining yourself in society and the real world is by being treated the same as everyone else. If you are treated differently, then you are set apart from other people. People should be considerate, open and understanding, but not make you their 'friend with OCD'.

I have an internal conflict within my head between the OCD and my desire to function. I have become increasingly skilled at shouting the OCD down and reducing its significance to me, though it still fights to be actioned. Therefore, I give OCD some small victories to enable the big victories for my desire to function as I want and need to.

I am a researcher by nature and have studied OCD in depth, which has helped me understand the processes which I have undergone and continue to go through. This has enabled me to manage my condition more effectively and feel less trapped by my thoughts and compulsions.

I would not get rid of my condition, just as I would not change any embarrassing moments or mistakes I have made. My condition is part of who I am and has made me the person I am today. I would not be a professional in healthcare or a confident adult if I had not experienced that which OCD has forced upon me. OCD has also made me able to confront and fight against obstacles in other areas of my life.

People with OCD should learn their own way of fighting against the OCD aspect of themselves, while accepting that it may never go away. Self-help books can give you a good starting point or booster when things are particularly difficult. Also, any goals you set yourself need to be realistic, such as 'today I will only check the door is locked 3 times' if you usually check 12 times.

People supporting people with OCD should allow the person with OCD to complete their rituals, but not engage themselves in them. They should instead continue the way they usually would and help the person with OCD focus on the world outside their own thoughts in between rituals, or on relatively good days.

CHAPTER 11

The Learning Environment

Teaching Approaches for Supporting Neuro-diversity

Many young people and adults with neuro-diverse conditions have great potential to achieve academically and have much to offer in terms of creativity and innovative perspectives. This can be hindered if teaching methods and environments do not support the weaker areas and differences of these learners. Although each of these conditions affects people in a different way, there are core areas that impact on most of the conditions in this book. This core consists of:

- information processing
- executive functioning (memory, organization and planning)
- social interaction
- sensory sensitivity
- anxiety and confidence.

Individualized support is essential for those with any disability or condition, but there are measures that can be taken as a basic standard for teaching and learning that will support all learners with all disabilities – and those without. If these measures are put in place, they will aid learning, increase access to the teaching and raise retention and achievement levels.

Considerations and strategies for teachers and learning support staff

As an educator, you have an important role to play as to whether this young person or adult completes their course and achieves what they are capable of. These young people are likely to have a history of negative school experiences, both socially and academically. These are not 'difficult' or 'challenging' learners; they have a condition which is legally considered to be a disability. The social model of disability states that it is society that disables the individual by not providing appropriate facilities and information, rather than the individual being disabled themselves. This is a useful model to consider when thinking about education; this is a person who has the intellectual ability to learn, but may need some small adjustments for them to access the learning environment – in the same way that a person who requires a wheelchair will need access to the physical environment.

Awareness training – for staff, learners and those with neuro-diverse conditions

Before we move on to approaches to meet these core needs, I want to say a few words about the importance of awareness training, not only for staff and for other learners, but also for those with these conditions. In my experience, we can be quite good at providing training for teaching and support staff working with diverse learning groups, but rarely do we spread that awareness to other students and to the individual with the condition themselves. It is my belief that bullying and exclusion usually happen because people see someone doing something 'weird', they don't know why and it scares them. This person becomes an easy target as they are different and do not fit in with everyone else. Generally, if we know why someone does what they do, we tend to be more forgiving and understanding because we know there is a reason, not just that they are being deliberately strange. Perhaps we should adopt a more open-minded policy even without the reason, but that is not always human nature. So, providing some general awareness training to other learners would be useful in raising awareness of the presence of learners with difference within the organization. If individual learners with neuro-diversity are happy to disclose their disabilities, they can participate in the training and give their own perspective on how they are affected. Fellow learners can then have the opportunity to ask questions. Depending on the maturity and ability level of the group, the information presented needs to be tailored to an appropriate depth and level. In my experience, this can work amazingly well and turn a bullied young person into one who the rest of the group sees as having useful skills and abilities.

The other person who requires information and awareness of neuro-diversity is the person with the condition. When I have spoken to young people about their diagnosis and what it means, overwhelmingly, they do not know. They have been told the name of the condition and no more. They have had no information or explanation about how they are different, or more importantly, how everyone else is different. If you are a minority living in a world that speaks a different language and has a whole different culture, you can feel very confused. You may assume that everyone is the same as you and feels the same way, but be confused as to why they seem to easily do things that you can't. This is how it can feel for people with neuro-diversity; their brains are wired to receive and decode information differently and so it can feel like living in a foreign land among people who don't share your view of the world. So, learning how the neuro-typical world (a term used to describe those without neuro-diverse conditions) operates is very useful for working out why things have been tough and why other people behave as they do. Learning about social expectations, the importance of non-verbal communication, punctuality, turning up with the correct books and completing the work required can be an eye-opener for a neuro-diverse person who may not have been able to access the correct information or instructions to perform well socially or academically and may have assumed that everyone else felt the same way. It can be a real light-bulb moment when someone understands why they have been inadvertently offending people or getting low grades due to misunderstandings or differences in interpretation of language or intention. Self-awareness and self-acceptance are very important for good self-esteem and confidence. An understanding of why you do what you do and your strengths and areas for development can have a huge impact on success and well-being. Basic awareness training for those with these conditions about their condition is important, but often neglected, work.

Information processing

- Use multi-sensory teaching approaches to ensure that learner's preferred learning method is utilized – visual, auditory, tactile, experiential.

- Do not make assumptions about ability: the learner is likely to have an uneven profile – high ability in some areas and considerably lower in others.

- Remember that ability may be higher than the person's written work conveys.

- Follow up verbal information with written or visual back-up.

- Provide course outline in advance to allow for preparation.

- Allow recording of lessons for learner to replay later.

- Break lessons into short activities.

- Break down information into small chunks.

- Understand that you may need to teach and reteach to embed.

- Use structural, sequential programmes that build on prior learning.

- Bloom's Taxonomy (Bloom 1956) is a model of cognitive learning processes, which states that more sophisticated cognitive learning cannot take place until lower level skills have been mastered. This is a helpful model for working with this type of learner.

- Make it clear at the start what the purpose of the lesson is and what learners are expected to know at the end of it. Review this at the end of the lesson.

- Use mind-maps (spider diagrams) to help visual learners organize thoughts.

- Allow interaction and involvement – passive listening is not an effective learning method for many people.

- Use clear sans serif fonts – size 12 or above.

- Do not write in red or green pens, which are hard for some learners to read.

Executive functioning – memory, organization and planning

- Provide a clear structure to the class and curriculum. Give learners a copy of this to aid planning and organization.

- Supply indicators of equipment and books required for each class. Some learners are unable to 'imagine' what they need to bring.

- Encourage the use of a diary, notebook and mobile phone reminders.

- Acknowledge that the person may have difficulty remembering days, weeks, months.

- Use colour coding to organize work.

- Be aware of direction confusion – left/right.

- Understand the person's page planning difficulties – they may not accurately estimate the space required.

- Have a clear, uncluttered page: leave plenty of space and use bullet points rather than blocks of text.

Social interaction

- Encourage social interaction between learners.

- Facilitate social activities and groups.

- Use mentoring and buddying schemes to ensure inclusion for those who find social interaction difficult.

- Model and teach appropriate social behaviour in a positive manner.

- Engage positively with learners with social skills issues – they may expect a negative response due to past experience.

- Realize that these learners are very likely to have been bullied – be aware of low self-esteem and confidence.

- Provide opportunities where they can excel – special interest groups and clubs, class presentations.

- Make sure all learners are contributing to group discussions – some may not be processing information quickly enough to keep up. Allow ten minutes at the end for additional comments to be made from anyone.

Sensory sensitivity

Environmental factors can have a big impact on some learners' ability to remain in the classroom long enough to learn.

- Remember that lighting is very important. Some learners with sensitivity to light can experience acute pain under certain types of light (fluorescent can be particularly bad). Flickering lights, poor lighting or very bright lights can bring on headaches and eye strain.

- Watch out for learners who rub their eyes or their head as if they have a headache.

- Provide an individual desk lamp as the main source of light for a learner: this can have a dramatic, positive effect, regardless of the quality of the lighting in the room.

- Use cream paper instead of white paper: this can reduce eye strain and glare for those who have visual sensitivity. This could be a cross-college policy and will not have a negative impact on other learners.

- Acknowledge that some people find filtering or prioritizing background noise very difficult and will be unable to hear the tutor if there is additional noise. Consider where the person is sitting in the room and how to minimize background noise.

- Understand that concentrating in a noisy environment can be difficult, so allow headphones, earplugs or personal music players when doing individual work.

- Allow regular breaks for moving around for those who find it hard to be still for long periods.

- Provide alternative assessment methods if writing or public speaking is part of person's disability.

Anxiety and confidence

There can be a tendency for these learners to be perfectionists and feel they have failed if they get something wrong.

- State clearly to all learners that mistakes are how we learn and improve.

- Reiterate that no one can be expected to know everything or understand everything immediately.

- Provide clear markers for adequate performance.

- Provide guidelines for expectations in terms of time and effort – learners may spend days on an assignment trying to make it perfect.

- Differentiate between different strengths of different learners – not everyone is good at everything.

- Emphasize that asking for help or working with others is a positive thing – some learners feel they must be able to do everything alone.

- Promote relaxation techniques – time in class for creating calm.

Considerations and strategies for individuals with neuro-diversity

- Do not be afraid to ask for learning support and adjustments. It is your right as a person with a disability.

- Learn as much as you can about how you are affected by your condition(s), so you can predict problematic situations in advance and organize ways to cope with them.

- Become self-aware about your weaker areas and find ways to overcome them.

- Use calendars, alarms, reminders and diaries to organize your timetable.

- Make lists of what equipment and books are required for each day so you do not forget.

- Request next week's lesson plans in advance so you have time to consider what will be required.

- Investigate eye tests, overlays and tinted glasses if you have headaches or visual discomfort.

- Eat, sleep and exercise well to ensure you have the best chance of keeping up with your studies. Avoid stimulants and processed food to maintain energy levels.

- Get clear and full guidance about what the programme will involve when choosing courses and subjects to study, – amount of contact time, presentations, written work, group work, etc. involved.

- Consider travelling methods and distances to college or university as this may cause additional stress at the beginning and end of each day.

- Don't forget that if you do not feel able to meet the requirements of the course, such as handing an essay in on time, make sure you tell your tutor as far in advance as possible. They will be more likely and able to extend the deadline if you do so.

- Remember it is never too late to return to study. Many people with neuro-diverse conditions, who were not diagnosed or supported at school when they were children, do very well when they return in later life.

CHAPTER 12

The Working Environment

Workplace Adjustments for Neuro-diverse Employees

As with schooling and education, the workplace can be a difficult place for some people with neuro-diversity. These are often skilled people, but who may have few qualifications and a poor or varied work history, neither of which are a fair reflection on the abilities and potential of the person. As we have seen in some of the personal accounts in previous chapters, poor achievements, low confidence and a late diagnosis often mean that people do not get the support and adjustments they need to reach that potential and remain in employment which works to their strengths. A lack of understanding from colleagues and employers, combined with a fear of looking 'stupid' or being found out, can result in bullying, being fired or the person walking out of their job rather than be 'discovered'.

Disclosure

For many people, disclosure of their condition is more likely to be an informal process, one to one with colleagues, rather than a management-led approach. There is undoubtedly an element of fear of the consequences in revealing one's true nature. Unfortunately, for many with neuro-diversity, whether disclosure is active or not, the individual may struggle to conceal their differences in a workplace which causes them stress and confusion. Not disclosing can mean that colleagues make assumptions about the reasons for certain behaviour ('weirdness' or 'stupidity', for example) and may react accordingly, which does not make the job any easier. Even if a disability is not disclosed at the time of recruitment, it can be done so at any point after the person has started work and the employer must accommodate the needs or the person. It is never too late to ask for adjustments to be made.

By disclosing a disability to an employer (or potential employer), you ensure that adequate support is provided as a preventative measure – before the stress or other problems arise. Also, there is the wider issue that if no one discloses, then awareness of the positive skills and abilities of those with neuro-diversity does not increase, which does not help those in the future seeking work.

Considerations and strategies for employers and support workers

Selecting and applying for work

- Possible unrealistic assessment of own abilities, over-estimating or underestimating strengths and areas for development.

- Lack of understanding of what a particular job role entails.

- Lack of motivation to work – may feel unable to manage work or have little interest in 'climbing the ladder'.

- Negative history of work experiences – low self-esteem.

- Difficulty planning and organizing self – meeting application deadlines.

- Literacy difficulties – some people struggle to articulate themselves despite high academic capability.

- Interacting – telephoning for more information regarding the job.

- Inability to 'lie', 'blag' or present self in best light on application form.

- Decision to disclose condition: the person may not have an official diagnosis or may fear discrimination.

Job applicant disclosure

As an employer, if a job applicant has disclosed a disability to you, you need to be aware of these issues and address them. Contacting the person before the interview and asking them what support they may need would be helpful. Provide detailed written information about what the interview process will involve, how long it will take and indications of the type of questions that will be asked. An interview should not be a test of interview skills, but a test of the skills required to do the job. A practical trial or test may be a better way of assessing this in someone who doesn't perform well with verbal expression or under pressure. This is a reasonable adjustment which does not discriminate on the grounds of a person's disability.

Interview issues

- Invisible conditions – lack of presentation of characteristics may hide difficulties or presentation may mask skills and abilities.

- Punctuality – person may struggle with concept of time.

- Open questions – 'Can you tell me how you feel about dealing with difficult people?' The person may not know what information is required, how much information or be able to relate to context of the job.

- Difference in eye contact and non-verbal skills can give a misleading impression of motivation.

- Inability to 'lie' and emphasize skills appropriate for the position.

- Reading and writing ability may not be a clear indicator of intelligence level.

- Environment may be a barrier to concentration and low arousal due to noise, lighting, distracting pictures, items or textures.

- Understanding the appropriate dress code.

- Difficulty reading or processing written information provided.

- Difficulty completing forms.

- Asking appropriate questions; not asking inappropriate questions.

- Talking too much or not enough.

- Short-term memory issues – forgetting interviewer's name, forgetting own work history.

- Motor difficulties – clumsiness.

- General anxiety and panic about making a good impression.

In the workplace

- Team-working – being required to see another's perspective and take this into consideration.

- Difficulties managing time and prioritizing.

- Accepting authority decisions regardless of own view.

- Social understanding – 'banter', pleasantries, reciprocity – making tea for everyone in the office in order to be part of group.

- Environmental sensitivity – temperature, noise, light, etc.

- Managing changes to structure, tasks, personnel and physical environment.

- Maintaining attention on routine and repetitive tasks.

- Attention to detail – may be more interested in outcome than quality of process.

- Procrastinating – hard to get started on projects.

- Oral instructions – may struggle to understand full extent of what is said.

- Incomplete or brief instructions where 'gaps' are to be filled by the person.

- Decision-making – difficult to see the consequences of unknown courses of action.

- May have difficulty eating or drinking with others – specific dietary habits.

- Processing complex information – may take more time.

- Difficulty expressing self verbally.

- Difficulty accepting feedback as this tends to be perceived as criticism.

- Being assertive.

Reasonable adjustments

- Undertake a job description analysis to identify areas of potential difficulty.

- Provide job and disability skills coaching for employee.

- Do not allow staff to undertake certain tasks which are not suited to their difficulties (e.g. data entry)

- Give overview and advance notice of complex tasks and don't ask people to multitask. It is difficult to structure and plan activities, especially in sequence.

- Write and produce documents using the spelling and grammar checks.

- Provide spell correctors, speech to text software or a buddy to assist proofreading.

- Back up lengthy information, whether oral or written documents, as people with neuro-diversity have difficulty holding and retaining linguistic information.

- Make written documents accessible through differentiation.

- Allow access to quiet environment or working from home, as it is difficult to concentrate in busy offices.

- Enable people to perform tasks in a suitable way at their own pace.

- Allow adequate time to prepare.

- Provide advanced organizers or holistic explanations first.

- Encourage discussion and reflection so that people are able to see the connections between tasks and the whole.

- Give out notes and agendas well in advance of meetings to allow people to prepare.

Support

- Use images and words on labels and colours to differentiate filing and administrative tasks.

- Provide specialist training on Q cards and memory aids if requiring staff to give oral presentations.

- Design templates and checklists to help staff remember everyday activities and procedures. Q cards are two-sided cards with categories or topics on one side and 5–9 bullet points (maximum 5–9 words each) on the other. They use as many senses as possible – colour, speech, movement and vision.

- Develop strategies to achieve tasks and pathways to end results.

- Make the connections between ideas explicit.

- Provide exemplars or models of different formats like letters and reports.

Assistive technology

Examples of assistive technology include:

- Reading pens. These pens run over text and 'speak' the words out loud. They can also give definitions of words to help with comprehension.

- Spell checkers and correctors. Spell checkers are commonly part of software in computer environments such as Windows. Spell correctors can help students 'guess' words they don't know all the letters of or are not sure how to spell. You can input your attempt (i.e. 'fonetic') and the spell corrector will try to find the word you mean. It will provide a list of possibles to choose from. It also helps with 'confusables' or homonyms which sound the same but are spelt differently and have different meanings (your and you're). An example is the Franklin Spell Corrector.

- Speech-to-text or text-to-speech software. Computer software which allows a person to dictate using their voice into the computer which then types their words (the programme has to be 'trained' to recognize a person's voice). An example is Dragon Naturally Speaking. Also available is text-to-speech which enables the computer to read back text to the user. An example is Read and Write Gold.

- Inspiration or other mind-mapping software. This is a computer software programme which enables people to make mind-maps or spider grams to collect and organize their thoughts and is very useful for those with dyslexia when planning essays or reports. An example is software supplied by Inspiration Software, Inc.

TechDis is an organization with much valuable information on technology and programme features to enhance accessibility for people with disabilities. Many things which they suggest do not even have financial implications. The JISC TechDis Service aims to be the leading educational advisory service, working across the UK, in the fields of accessibility and inclusion. See the Resources section at the end of the book for details of companies which supply this technology.

Equipment

- Overlays and screen guards can reduce visual difficulties.
- Ergonomic assessment can ensure environmental comfort.

- Digital recorders can record messages or lengthy information.

- Memory aids, personal organizers and mobile phones can assist organization and timekeeping.

What if you suspect an employee has a neuro-diverse condition?

If an employee has not disclosed and yet you suspect that they have some form of neuro-diversity and it is causing them problems at work that you cannot ignore, what do you do?

This is a very difficult and sensitive situation, which needs to be handled with care. I have had a number of employers contact me regarding a staff member who they believe is affected by neuro-diversity, asking me what they should do. It is important to remember that these conditions can be assessed or diagnosed only by a qualified practitioner, so any suggestion of a disability must be aired with great caution, if at all. The approach you use depends on whether you feel that the person is aware that they have difficulties and what kind of working relationship you have with them.

- Can you deal with the job-related issues without mentioning your suspicions of neuro-diversity?

- What is your motivation for telling someone that you believe they have a neuro-diverse condition?

- Will it help this person to know? If so, in what ways?

- What will happen if the person rejects your suggestions or is very offended?

If you are determined that the subject needs to be tackled with the employee and they want to air their thoughts, it is recommended that you do so in an informal, private and relaxed conversation in which you casually mention that you have read something about the condition involved and can see aspects of that in the employee. Alternatively, you could ask the employee if they would be willing to have a chat to a specialist who may be able to give a more informed opinion. It is important that the person understands that you are willing to support them to be able to complete their work and provide the adjustments required for them to do so. This is a very delicate matter and extreme caution must be exercised to adhere to appropriate legal and ethical guidelines and procedures when approaching an employee.

If the employee agrees that they may have a condition, you must then provide support in accessing a diagnosis (if one is required), training staff, providing a mentor or other specialist support and ensuring that the workplace meets the needs of the individual.

Things to consider by the employer

- Due to the nature of neuro-diversity and issues around concentration and attention, it is especially important for the person to have some level of interest in the work. The person may find it impossible to do any random job assigned to them.

- A structured, regular, scheduled meeting time would provide a recognizable, appropriate place for discussions about performance or other work issues.

- The person with neuro-diversity may find it difficult to assess their own abilities and limitations and may agree to take on roles and responsibilities that they do not understand.

- High qualifications and/or an impressive CV may not be

an accurate measure of whether someone can cope socially or flexibly in a work environment.

- Low or non-existent qualifications and/or a poor CV may not be an accurate measure of intelligence or ability.

- Find another way to assess someone's abilities relating to the actual task that they will be required to carry out instead of or as well as an interview. Asking someone with a verbal communication difference to verbally express their skills and abilities is discriminating on the grounds of their disability. A person with a visual impairment would not be asked to represent themselves visually. This is the same principle.

- If someone is behaving in a way that you consider to be unusual, ask them why. Generally, people don't mind being asked in the spirit of enquiry. This is better than making assumptions about a person's behaviour which may be wrong.

- In exchange for certain skills, there may be limitations in others. Everybody has their strengths and deserves support with their weaker areas.

- If a person has experienced bullying in a social situation, it will take some time before they can trust that any new interaction or association will not be the same.

- Be direct with instructions and requirements. Do not wrap up the message with meaningless words. Keep it brief and clear, allowing for no misinterpretations. Back up with written reminders.

- Some people can work very quickly and may need constant challenges to keep their interest. Boredom will lead to lack of motivation and effort.

- When explaining a task, provide the bigger picture. If a person can see where the part of the job they are doing fits into the whole project, this will improve understanding and motivation. If someone perceives their job to be pointless (because no one has explained the point) they may quickly tire.

- Provide a suitable workspace, which may be facing a wall or in a separate room. If possible, allow the person to keep the same workspace and not have to use any available desk.

- Be aware that some people may ruminate and go over situations and conversations in their head many times. What may have seemed to be a trivial exchange to you may cause anxiety and worry over a much longer period of time for them.

- Be open to the possibility that although it may be unusual, the person may have good ideas and a unique slant to solving problems. Always be willing to reserve judgement.

- Identify tasks which the person can excel at and do the same for all other members of staff.

Considerations and strategies for individuals with neuro-diversity

Searching for employment

Here are some questions to consider when looking for work which suits your strengths and requirements:

- What do you think would be your ideal job?
- How many hours per week or per day do you feel you would be able to work?

- How far away from home could you travel?
- Do you want to work outdoors or indoors?
- What type of environment would you prefer to work in – shop, restaurant, office, factory, teaching, outdoors, driving?
- What physical or sensory factors would you need to consider (noise, lighting, etc.)?
- How much do you need to earn? Can you work out how much it costs you to live?
- What type of tasks would you want to be doing?
- Are you happy meeting new people, speaking at meetings and using the telephone?
- Do you enjoy flexible and changing work or a predictable workload?
- Will the requirement for reading, writing and/or maths be a problem?
- What qualifications would you need to obtain to be able to do this job? If you don't have the qualifications, how could you persuade a company that you can do the job?
- Would you be willing to study in your spare time to gain qualifications?
- Would you prefer to work alone or as part of a team?
- Would you want to be responsible for staff?
- What support would you need when writing a CV, telephoning the company for an application form, attending an interview or in on-the-job support?

Interview tips

- Be on time (or early) – this is very important. Lateness is likely to be seen as a sign of lack of interest in the job, or lack of motivation.

- Practise the route and journey beforehand to ensure you have left yourself enough time.

- Shower, shave, wash and brush hair, wear clean, smart clothes and smart shoes. Try to look your best as these things often matter to those interviewing you.

- Remember that everyone gets nervous and anxious about job interviews – this is a normal and reasonable reaction.

- Learn about the company and the job so you can ask questions and show that you have done your research – this shows that you are keen and interested.

- If you don't understand a question, ask politely for it to be rephrased.

- Try to retain concentration on what the interviewer is saying.

- If you need to take a five-minute break to maintain attention, ask to do so.

- Usually more than a one-word answer is required as the interviewer will want you to give an example or details relating to the questions.

- Generally an answer which involves you talking for five minutes or more is too long.

- Stay focused on the question and do not go off track and talk about other things.

- Do not say anything negative about the job or the company, even if you think it.

- Prepare some things to say which make you sound enthusiastic about working for the company.

- Remember that an interview is a test of how well the interviewer thinks you can do the job and how well you will fit in with the company and you only have a limited amount of time to do this, so use it well.

Things to consider for individuals with neuro-diversity

- Having a good knowledge and awareness of your condition and how it affects you can be very helpful in being able to ask for what you need.

- Always consider the physical environment (noise, light, smell, etc.) to be a potential stressor if you feel unable to cope at work. Keep a diary to try to isolate the cause of your discomfort, if it is not immediately obvious. It may be that on certain days, someone wears a perfume that gives you headaches, for example.

- If you do not wish to 'disclose' officially, it can be easy to get small adjustments without mentioning your condition. If you cannot work in a noisy environment, for example, you can say: 'I work much better in a quieter environment, so I'm going to put these earplugs in/listen to some music/ move my desk over there'. People are very accepting of this type of assertiveness.

- Consider how you will travel to a job when applying. Will you be able to make the journey to work and not be too exhausted or stressed when you arrive? Practise the journey to see how long it takes and what it involves.

- Consider presentation and personal hygiene. Look in magazines and watch how people dress when they are going to work. It is very important to wear the appropriate clothing for the job and wash and change it regularly.

- Don't be afraid to ask your employer for support if you feel overwhelmed. They are legally obliged to help you and provide what you need (within reason). Find an advocate or get some legal advice if you feel you need it.

- Learning about yourself and recognizing the triggers for stress and overload can be very useful in being able to take some time out when you feel these occurring.

- Success or failure in getting a job is only a matter of how good the other applicants were. Most people apply for many jobs that they don't get. It doesn't mean that you are a failure or that you will never get a job. Ask for feedback from the interviewer(s) as to how you could improve your performance.

- Interviews are fake situations. They are not real conversations; they are more like a test in which the correct answers to the questions are not always obvious. Working out what is required can be very difficult. Reading as much about the job roles and organization as possible may help to give you an idea of the type of company it is – whether they are informal and dynamic or more traditional and structured. This may give you clues as to the type of person they are looking to 'fit' in.

References

American Psychiatric Association (APA) (1994) *Diagnostic and Statistical Manual of Mental Disorders*, 4th edn (DSM-IV). Washington, DC: APA.

Anderson, A. (2009) *History of Anxiety Disorders*. Available at http://anxiety-panic.com/history, accessed 6 July 2009.

Attwood, T. (2006) *The Complete Guide to Asperger's Syndrome*. London: Jessica Kingsley Publishers.

Balaban, C.D. and Thayer, J.F. (2001) 'Neurological bases for balance–anxiety links.' *Journal of Anxiety Disorders 15*, 1–2, 53–79.

Baron-Cohen, S. (2004) *The Essential Difference*. London: Penguin.

Bloom, B.S. (ed.) (1956) *Taxonomy of Educational Objectives: The Classification of Educational Goals – Handbook I: Cognitive Domain*. New York: McKay.

Blume, H. (1998) 'Neurodiversity.' *The Atlantic*. Available at www.theatlantic.com/doc/199809u/neurodiversity, accessed on 6 July 2009.

Box, H. (ed.) (2008) 'Tourette Syndrome – An Introduction.' *Tourettes Action*. Available at www.tourettes-action.org.uk/storage/Tourette%20Syndrome%20-%20an%20introduction.pdf

Brayton, H. (1997) 'Listening to students with specific learning difficulties in colleges of FE.' *Skill Journal 58*, 1–16.

Bynner, S. and Parsons, J. (1997) *Does Numeracy Matter? Evidence from the National Child Development Study on the Impact of Poor Numeracy on Adult Life*. London: The Basic Skills Agency.

Carter, R. (1998) *Mapping the Mind*. London: Weidenfeld & Nicolson.

Colley, M. (2006) *Living with Dyspraxia: A Guide for Adults with Developmental Dyspraxia*. London: Jessica Kingsley Publishers.

Dare, R.C., Heyman, I., Giovannoni, G. and Church A.J. (2005) 'Incidence of anti-brain antibodies in children with obsessive-compulsive disorder.' *British Journal of Psychiatry 187*, 314–319.

Davis, R.D. (1994) *The Gift of Dyslexia*. London: Souvenir Press.

Department for Education and Skills (DfES) (2001) *Guidance to Support Pupils with Dyslexia and Dyscalculia.* London: DfES.

Department for Education and Skills (DfES) (2004) *A Framework for Understanding Dyslexia: Information on Theories and Approaches to Dyslexia and Dyscalculia.* London: Department for Education and Skills. Crown Copyright.

Dyslexia Initiative Conference (2002) *Realising potential through communication.* Oxford 2002.

Esquirol, J.E. (1838) *Des maladies mentales: A Treatise on Insanity.* Philadelphia, PA: Lea & Blanchard.

Fireman, B., Koran, L.M., Leventhal, J.L. and Jacobson, A. (2001) 'The prevalence of clinically recognized obsessive-compulsive disorder in a large health maintenance organization.' *American Journal of Psychiatry 158*, 11, 1904–1910.

Frith, U. (1997) 'Brain, Mind and Behaviour.' In C. Hulme and M. Snowling (eds) *Dyslexia, Biology, Cognition and Interventions.* London: Whurr.

Frith, U. (2008) *Autism: A Very Short Introduction.* Oxford: Oxford University Press.

Ghaziuddin, M. (2005) *Mental Health Aspects of Autism and Asperger Syndrome.* London: Jessica Kingsley Publishers.

Gubbay, S.S. (1975) *The Clumsy Child: A Study of Developmental Apraxia and Agnostic Ataxia.* London: Saunders.

Hale, A. (1997) 'ABC of mental health: Anxiety.' *British Medical Journal 314*, 1886–1889.

Hendrickx, S. (2008) *Asperger Syndrome and Employment: What People with Asperger Syndrome Really Really Want.* London: Jessica Kingsley Publishers.

Hinshelwood, J. (1896) 'A case of dyslexia: A peculiar form of word-blindness.' *The Lancet 2*, 1451–1454.

Hinshelwood, J. (1917) *Congenital Word-Blindness.* London: H.K. Lewis.

Jasper, L. and Goldberg, I. (1993) *Adult ADD Screening Test.* Version 5.0. Available at http://users.rcn.com/peregrin.enteract/add/addtest.txt, accessed 6 July 2009.

King, R. and Leckman, J. (2004) 'Tic Disorders.' In J. Wiener and R. Dulcan (eds) *Textbook of Child and Adolescent Psychiatry*, 3rd edn. Arlington, VA: American Psychiatric Publishing.

Kosc, L. (1974) *Developmental dyscalculia. Journal of Learning Disabilities 7*, 3, 164–177.

Kutscher, M.L. (2005) *Kids in the Syndrome Mix of ADHD, LD, Asperger's, Tourette's, Bipolar, and More!* London: Jessica Kingsley Publishers.

Mental Health Foundation (2006) *Cheers? Understanding the Relationship between Alcohol and Mental Health.* London: Mental Health Foundation.

Morgan, E. and Klein, C. (2000) *The Dyslexic Adult in a Non-Dyslexic World.* London: Whurr.

National Health Service Choices (2008) *Attention Deficit Hyperactivity Disorder: Symptoms of ADHD.* London: NHS. Available at www.nhs.uk/Conditions/Attention-deficit-hyperactivity-disorder/Pages/Symptoms.aspx?url=Pages/What-is-it.aspx&r=1&rtitle=Attention+deficit+hyperactivity+disorder+-+Symptoms, accessed 6 July 2009.

National Institute for Health and Clinical Excellence (NICE) (2008) *NICE Guidelines: Attention Deficit Hyperactivity Disorder.* London: NICE. Available at www.nice.org.uk/nicemedia/pdf/ADHDFullGuideline.pdf, accessed 6 July 2009.

OCD-UK (2009) 'What is Obsessive-Compulsive Disorder?' Available at www.ocduk.org/1/ocd, accessed 30 September 2009.

Office for National Statistics (ONS) (2000) *Psychiatric Morbidity among Adults Living in Private Households in Great Britain.* London: ONS.

Orton, S.T. (1937) *Reading, Writing and Speech Problems in Children.* New York: Norton.

Packer, L.E. (1998) *A Primer on Tics and Tourette's Including Life Span Changes, Psychosocial Consequences, the Role of Stress, and Much More.* Available at www.tourettesyndrome.net/tourette_primer.htm, accessed 6 July 2009.

Palmer, E.D. and Finger, S. (2001) 'An early description of ADHD (Inattentive Subtype): Dr Alexander Crichton and "Mental Restlessness" (1798).' *Child and Adolescent Mental Health* 6, 2, 66–73.

Parliamentary Office of Science and Technology (2004) 'Dyslexia and dyscalculia.' *Postnote* 226.

Pauc, R. (2008) *Could It Be You? Overcoming Dyslexia, Dyspraxia, ADHD, OCD, Tourette's Syndrome, Autism and Asperger Syndrome in Adults.* London: Virgin.

Peterson, B.S. (2001) 'Neuroimaging Studies of Tourette Syndrome: A Decade of Progress.' In D.J. Cohen, J. Jankovic and C.G. Goetz (eds) *Tourette Syndrome.* Philadelphia, PA: Lippincott Williams & Wilkins.

Peterson, B.S. and Leckman, J.F. (1998) 'The temporal dynamics of tics in Gilles de la Tourette syndrome.' *Biological Psychiatry 44*, 12, 1337–1348.

Porter, P. (1997) *Medicine, A History of Healing: Ancient Traditions to Modern Practices.* New York: Ivy Press.

Portwood, M. (1999) *Developmental Dyspraxia: Identification and Intervention: A Manual for Parents and Professionals*, 2nd edn. London: David Fulton.

Searight, H.R., Burke, J.M. and Rottnek, F. (2000) 'Adult ADHD: Evaluation and treatment in family medicine.' *American Family Physician 62*, 2, 2077–2086, 2091–2092.

Shaywitz, S. (1996) 'Dyslexia.' *Scientific American 275*, 98–104.

Shorter, E. (1997) *A History of Psychiatry: From the Era of the Asylum to the Age of Prozac.* London: Wiley.

Snowling, M. and Stackhouse, J. (2000) *Dyslexia, Speech and Language.* London: Whurr.

Stein, J. (2001) 'The magnocellular theory of developmental dyslexia.' *Dyslexia: An International Journal 7*, 12–36.

Stephenson, L. and Fairgrieve, E. (1996) 'Dyslexia and the Links with Motor Problems.' In G. Reid (ed.) *Dimensions of Dyslexia: Literacy, Language and Learning*, Volume 2. Edinburgh: Moray House.

Thompson, M.E. and Watkins, E.J. (1996) *Dyslexia: A Teaching Handbook.* London: Whurr.

Tinsley, M. and Hendrickx, S. (2008) *Asperger Syndrome and Alcohol: Drinking to Cope?* London: Jessica Kingsley Publishers.

Tourettes Action (2009) *History of Tourette Syndrome.* Available at www.whonamedit.com/synd.cfm/1549.html, accessed 21 September 2009.

World Health Organization (WHO) (1994) *International Statistical Classification of Diseases and Related Health Problems*, 10th Revision (ICD-10). Geneva: WHO.

Further Reading

Neuro-diversity

Ottinger, B. (2003) *Tictionary – A Reference Guide to the World of Tourette Syndrome, Asperger Syndrome, Attention Deficit Hyperactivity Disorder and Obsessive-Compulsive Disorder for Parents and Professionals*. London: Jessica Kingsley Publishers.

Pauc, R. (2008) *Could It Be You? Overcoming Dyslexia, Dyspraxia, ADHD, OCD, Tourette's Syndrome, Autism and Asperger Syndrome in Adults*. London: Virgin.

Attention deficit hyperactivity disorder and attention deficit disorder

Kolberg, J. and Nadeau, K. (2002) *ADD-Friendly Ways to Organize Your Life*. New York: Brunner-Routledge.

Patterson, K. (2004) *ADD and Me: Forty Years in a Fog*. London: Jessica Kingsley Publishers.

Autistic spectrum and Asperger syndrome

Attwood, T. (2006) *The Complete Guide to Asperger's Syndrome*. London: Jessica Kingsley Publishers.

Hendrickx, S. (2008) *Asperger Syndrome and Employment: What People with Asperger Syndrome Really Really Want*. London: Jessica Kingsley Publishers.

Perry, N. (2008) *Adults on the Autism Spectrum Leave the Nest: Achieving Supported Independence*. London: Jessica Kingsley Publishers.

Dyslexia

Chivers, M. (2001) *Practical Strategies for Living with Dyslexia*. London: Jessica Kingsley Publishers.

Morgan, E. and Klein, C. (2000) *The Dyslexic Adult in a Non-dyslexic World*. London: Whurr.

Dyspraxia

Biggs, V. (2005) *Caged in Chaos: A Dyspraxic Guide to Breaking Free*. London: Jessica Kingsley Publishers.

Colley, M. (2006) *Living with Dyspraxia: A Guide for Adults with Developmental Dyspraxia*. London: Jessica Kingsley Publishers.

Kirby, A. (2003) *The Adolescent with Developmental Co-ordination Disorder (DCD)*. London: Jessica Kingsley Publishers.

Anxiety disorders

Beck, A.T., Emery, G. and Greenberg, R. (1985) *Anxiety Disorders and Phobias: A Cognitive Perspective*. New York: Basic Books.

Bourne, E.J. (2005) *The Anxiety and Phobia Workbook*, 4th edn. Oakland, CA: New Harbinger.

Ingham, C. (2000) *Panic Attacks: What They Are, Why They Happen, and What You Can Do about Them*. London: Thorsons.

Obsessive-compulsive disorder

Deane, R. (2005) *Washing My Life Away: Surviving Obsessive-Compulsive Disorder*. London: Jessica Kingsley Publishers.

Hyman, B.M. and DuFrene, T. (2008) *Coping with OCD: Practical Strategies for Living Well with Obsessive-Compulsive Disorder*. Oakland, CA: New Harbinger.

Cognitive behavioural therapy

Burns, D.D. (1999) *The Feeling Good Handbook*. New York: Plume.

Jeffers, S. (2007) *Feel the Fear and Do It Anyway*. London: Vermilion.

Seiler, L. (2008) *Cool Connections with Cognitive Behavioural Therapy: Encouraging Self-esteem, Resilience and Well-being in Children and Young People Using CBT Approaches*. London: Jessica Kingsley Publishers.

Willson, R. and Branch, R. (2005) *Cognitive Behavioural Therapy for Dummies*. Chichester: Wiley.

Resources

The Internet is full of information, resources and publications on all the conditions featured in this book. For all of these conditions, there are online questionnaires, which can provide an indication of whether a full assessment should be sought. Most of the websites in this section will have such information on them. If not, contact them and they should be able to tell you where to find it.

All websites were accessed on 7 July 2009.

Neuro-diversity

Brain.HE (Best Resources for Achievement and Intervention re Neurodiversity in Higher Education)
www.brainhe.com
Information resource for staff and students in higher education affected by neuro-diversity or supporting those who are

Developmental Adult Neuro-Diversity Association (DANDA)
www.danda.org.uk
UK-based awareness-raising organization for all neuro-diverse conditions

Learning Disabilities Association of America
www.ldanatl.org
Lots of information for professionals and individual on all the conditions in this book

Neurodiversity Weblog
www.neurodiversity.com/main.html
Opinions, articles and information

Attention deficit hyperactivity disorder and attention deficit disorder

About.com: ADD/ADHD
http://add.about.com
Information about all aspects of ADHD and ADD

Adult Attention Deficit Disorder – UK (AADD-UK) www.aadd.org.uk
A list of UK-based specialist clinicians, online forum and general information about ADHD in adults

Attention Deficit Disorder Association www.add.org
Support groups, articles and information

Autistic spectrum and Asperger syndrome

Asperger's Syndrome Foundation www.aspergerfoundation.org.uk
Organization providing seminars on Asperger syndrome for individuals, family members and professionals in London, also has information sheets and email enquiry service

Tony Attwood www.tonyattwood.com.au
Australian-based world authority on Asperger syndrome and very nice man

Australian Advisory Board on Autism Spectrum Disorders www.autismaus.com.au
Members' organization representing individuals with autism and their families

Autism Canada Foundation www.autismcanada.org
Resources, information and conferences in Canada

Autism Society of America (ASA) www.autism-society.org
Local groups across the USA, information and conferences about autism, including Asperger syndrome

Hendrickx Associates www.asperger-training.com
Provides training, assessments and consultancy in autism, Asperger syndrome, dyslexia and general neuro-diversity

National Autistic Society (NAS) www.nas.org.uk
Provides services, helplines, training, information sheets and an online directory of all autism and Asperger syndrome related services in the UK

OASIS (Online Asperger Syndrome Information and Support) www.aspergersyndrome.org
Articles, book reviews and an online members' forum for adults with Asperger syndrome

Dyslexia

British Dyslexia Association (BDA) www.bdadyslexia.org.uk
Offers training, self-assessment tests, information and accreditation to dyslexia-friendly organizations, also has dyscalculia information

Dyslexia Action www.dyslexiaaction.org.uk
Accredited training courses, information and assessments

Dyslexia Adults www.dyslexia-adults.com
US-based site with forum and information for adults with dyslexia

Dyslexia Unlocked www.dyslexia-unlocked.com
Claire Salter's specialist dyslexia training, support and assessment consultancy, based in UK

The Whole Dyslexia Society (Canada) www.dyslexiacanada.com
Supporting those with dyslexia

Dyspraxia

Dyspraxia Foundation www.dyspraxiafoundation.org.uk
Information, lists of groups and conferences for those with dyspraxia and professionals, based in UK

Dyspraxia Inclusive Training
www.dyspraxia-training.co.uk
UK-based training provider run by Janet
Taylor, a woman with dyspraxia, offering specialist courses to educational establishments
and employers

Dyspraxia USA
www.dyspraxiausa.org
Forum and resources including sections on
adults' dyspraxia

Tourette syndrome

Tourettes Action – Statistics
www.tourettes-action.org.uk/statistics
Tourette Syndrome support charity providing
a helpline, research and information

Tourette Syndrome Association of Australia
www.tourette.org.au
Non-profit organization supporting people
with TS

Tourette Syndrome Association USA
www.tsa-usa.org
Conferences, research and information on TS

Tourette Syndrome Foundation of Canada
www.tourette.ca
Non-profit organization assisting people
with TS

Anxiety disorders

Anxiety Disorders Association of America
(ADAA)
www.adaa.org
Support, therapist list and conferences

Anxiety Disorders Association of Canada
(ADAC)
www.anxietycanada.ca
Awareness, prevention and treatment of anxiety disorders

Anxiety-Panic.com
www.anxiety-panic.com
Website with full history of anxiety disorders

Anxiety UK (formerly National Phobics
Society)
www.anxietyuk.org.uk
Research opportunities, information on a
wide range of anxiety disorders, helpline, private and NHS services available and treatment
information

OCD-UK
www.ocduk.org
OCD support organization providing fact
sheets, support strategies, training and helpline

Panic Anxiety Disorder Association (PADA)
of Australia
www.panicanxietydisorder.org.au/index.htm
Helpline, information and training for those
with anxiety and professionals

Assistive Technology Suppliers

Franklin
www.franklin.com
Suppliers of innovative electronic language
learning solutions, such as the Franklin Spell
Corrector

Inspiration Software, Inc.
www.inspiration.com
Suppliers of inspiration and other mind-mapping software

JISC TechDis
www.techdis.ac.uk
Educational advisory service, providing expert
guidance on disability and technology

Nuance Communications UK
www.nuance.com
Suppliers of speech-to-text software, such as
Dragon Naturally Speaking

TechReady
www.teachready.co.uk
Suppliers of text-to-speech software, such as
Read and Write Gold

Index